PASSAGES: KEY M

The Perry Expedition and the "Opening of Japan to the West," 1853–1873

A Short History with Documents

PASSAGES: KEY MOMENTS IN HISTORY

The Perry Expedition and the "Opening of Japan to the West," 1853–1873

A Short History with Documents

Paul H. Clark

Hackett Publishing Company, Inc.
Indianapolis/Cambridge

Printed in the United States of America

23 22 21 20 1 2 3 4 5 6 7

For further information, please address
Hackett Publishing Company, Inc.
P.O. Box 44937
Indianapolis, Indiana 46244-0937

www.hackettpublishing.com

Cover design by Rick Todhunter
Interior design by Laura Clark
Composition by Aptara, Inc.

Library of Congress Control Number: 2019953835

ISBN-13: 978-1-62466-889-0 (cloth)
ISBN-13: 978-1-62466-886-9 (pbk.)

The paper used in this publication meets the minimum requirements of American National Standard for Information Sciences—Permanence of Paper for Printed Library Materials, ANSI Z39.48–1984.

∞

CONTENTS

PREFACE

The rumors and fragmentary reports were true. The Council of Elders in Japan had been warned by the Dutch and the Ryūkyū islanders that U.S. President Millard Fillmore (1800–1874) was determined to force the Japanese government to end its policy of national seclusion. But Japan's leaders hoped it would not happen soon. Nonetheless, Commodore Matthew Perry's squadron of four ships sailed unbidden into Tokyo Bay on July 8, 1853. Perry had been instructed by President Fillmore to be polite and careful, but he was not to be delayed or denied. Abe Masahiro (1819–1857), the leader of the Council of Elders, hoped that he could treat the United States as Japan had treated all other Western nations. For the past two centuries, the Japanese had used tried-and-true delaying tactics—threats, obfuscation, misdirection, and, on rare occasions, opening fire on unwelcome ships—to keep the curious, and even most of the desperate, foreigners away. It was not a shock to the Japanese that the Americans had come; nor were Japan's leaders heedless of the dangers faced by the country. But the appearance of the so-called Black Ships (steam-driven) of Commodore Perry's squadron indicated that this visit might be different. In years past, the vastness of the Pacific Ocean had meant that most threats to Japan had come only from the south and west. The United States hadn't been much of a concern for most of its existence and posed little threat to Japan's security, so long as North America's western coast was only sparsely populated. All that changed, however, in the 1840s when the dispute over the Oregon Territory was settled with Great Britain and when California became a state in 1850. The United States had become a Pacific power in a very short period of time, and Japan's diplomatic situation suddenly got a lot more complicated.

The Council of Elders were also not surprised that the Westerners were becoming more assertive. They had observed the effects of the First Opium War (1839–1842) on China and were acutely conscious of just how dangerous Great Britain, in particular, had become. Japan's leaders were aware that industrialization had had a multiplying effect on Britain's military and that Japan could be in big trouble if even just a few of these modern ships appeared off their coast. Given that the United States, France, and the Netherlands (among others) had also begun the process of industrialization, it was only a matter of time before they began to act in a fashion similar to Great Britain. Though Japan's leaders intended to try to rebuff the industrialized West using their standard tactics, they understood that such efforts might be unsuccessful this time.

The search for solutions that would work for Japan as its leaders tried to secure its borders during the 1850s and 1860s was much more problematic than identifying its vulnerabilities. To succeed, Japan would need to undergo a series of painful reforms. All serious efforts at reform bring uncertainty and risk, and this would have been a time fraught with peril even if the Japanese government enjoyed the goodwill and support of the population. Unfortunately for Japan, the Tokugawa system of government was authoritarian in nature and explicitly forbade the vast majority of the population from participating in public life. To meet the challenges posed by industrialization and a resurgent West, Japan's leaders needed to mobilize the entire population behind the movement to reform the country. Given the structural weakness of the Tokugawa regime, and the erosion of public support for the government in the previous decades, this was not possible. Once reform was initiated, and the authoritarian government's weaknesses exposed, its opponents were emboldened and moved against it; the more daring of these opponents took up arms and openly rebelled.

This is the story of Japan as it sought to deal with a series of challenges posed by the visits of Commodore Perry. It is important to note that the Japanese government was dealing with much more than just a determined United States. Over the course of a few short months, it had to cope with intrusions by the French, the Russians, the Dutch, and the British. These Western imperialists had the power and the means to force Japan into the kinds of treaties that would effectively spell the end of Japan's autonomy, and maybe even its existence as an independent country. Meanwhile, in those same months, Japan was also faced with a serious insurrection, the death of an emperor, and the death of a shogun—as well as with a series of natural disasters and associated famines. It was a perfect storm of catastrophes.

Chapter One of this book introduces and describes the Tokugawa system of government. Included is a brief description of the organizational structure of the shogunate, the structure of Japanese society at this moment in time, and some of the emblematic policies that characterized the Early Modern epoch in the country. This is followed by a brief snapshot of the domestic situation in Japan in the years leading up to the visits by Commodore Perry. Finally, this chapter describes the nature of "gunboat diplomacy" and the early efforts of Europeans to normalize relations with Japan. The principal goal of Chapter Two is to detail the actual visits of Commodore Perry's squadron, the initial responses to his visit by the Japanese, and the efforts of the European powers to also sign agreements with the Japanese as soon as possible. Along the way, an outline of some of the most well-known visits, or attempted visits, to Japan by the Western nations in the two decades before Commodore Perry's visits will provide contrast to the actual Perry visits. Chapter Three outlines the primary consequences of Commodore Perry's visit to Japan. Included is a chronicle of the rise of serious opposition to the government, the collapse of the Tokugawa shogunate, and the Boshin War (1868–1869) that permanently ended the feudal age. Chapter Four highlights the Meiji Restoration and efforts of the new Japanese leadership to create a government, initiate comprehensive reforms, and begin to address some of the country's most pressing international problems.

ACKNOWLEDGMENTS

I have incurred many personal and professional debts as this book has taken shape. I would like to thank the team at Hackett Publishing Company for their support and forbearance. In particular, I am grateful to Rick Todhunter for inviting me to write this book, for his patience, and for his many astute comments in the writing process. Two anonymous readers also provided insightful remarks that have helped me refine the book. I wish to thank my colleagues in the Department of History at West Texas A&M University for allowing me to bounce ideas off of them and for helping to create an environment at a teaching institution where scholarship and creative thinking are highly valued. This project was also supported, in part, by a grant from the West Texas A&M University Foundation Development Endowment. I thank them for their support.

It would be difficult to overstate the importance of my spouse and unofficial editor, Elizabeth Morrow Clark, in the successful completion of this book. From beginning to end, her support, comments, and editing have enriched the work and made it more meaningful. I thank her and my three children—Katherine, Charlotte, and Phillip—for their forbearance and for making it all worthwhile. Though many have assisted me in ways too numerous to mention, I am, of course, solely responsible for the errors and omissions in the work.

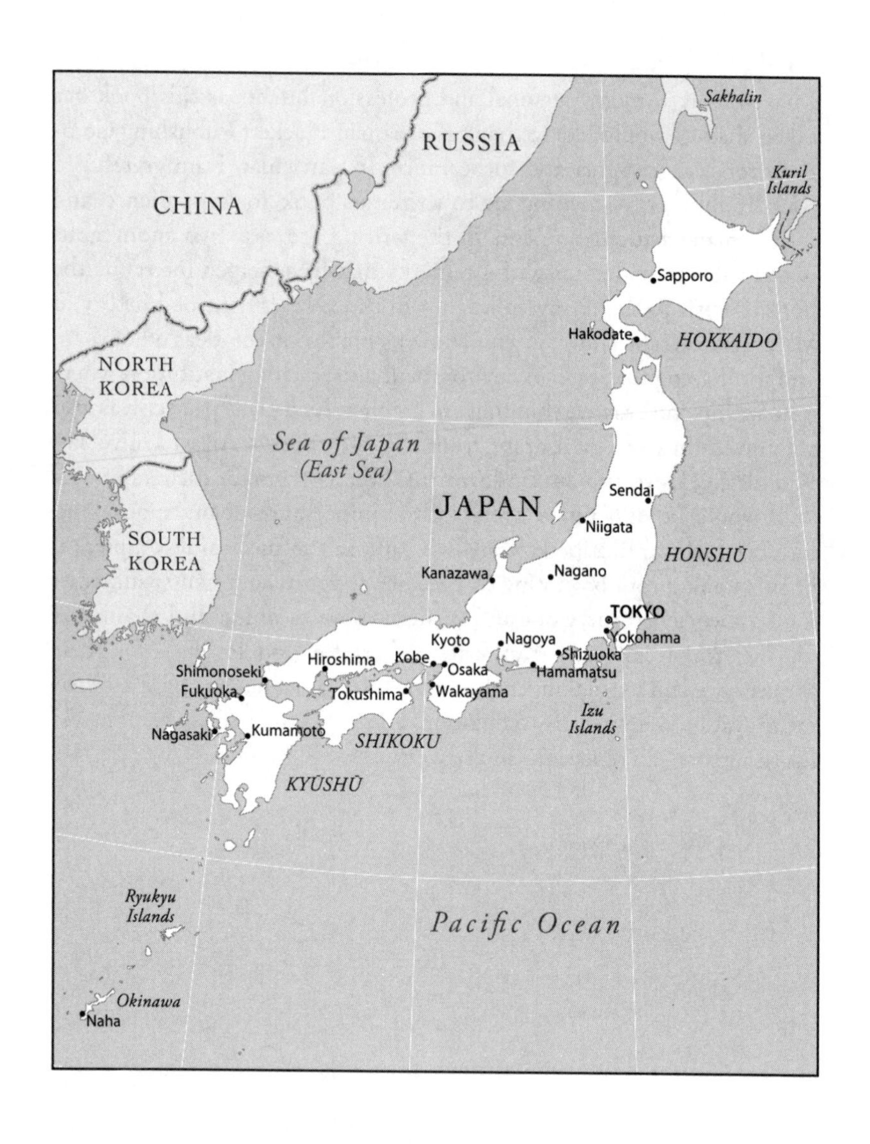
RUSSIA
CHINA
Sakhalin
Kuril Islands
Sapporo
Hakodate
HOKKAIDO
NORTH KOREA
Sea of Japan
(East Sea)
JAPAN
Sendai
Niigata
SOUTH KOREA
HONSHŪ
Kanazawa
Nagano
TOKYO
Yokohama
Kyoto
Nagoya
Shizuoka
Hiroshima
Kobe
Osaka
Hamamatsu
Shimonoseki
Fukuoka
Tokushima
Wakayama
Izu Islands
Nagasaki
Kumamoto
SHIKOKU
KYŪSHŪ
Ryukyu Islands
Pacific Ocean
Okinawa
Naha

CHRONOLOGY

1600	Battle of Sekigahara (Tokugawa period begins)
1603	Tokugawa Ieyasu officially becomes shogun; abdicates in favor of his son in 1605
1605	Tokugawa Hidetada becomes shogun; abdicates in favor of his son in 1623
1623–1651	Period of Tokugawa Iemitsu shogunate
1635	Policy of *sankin kōtai* introduced (great lords required to live in Edo in alternate years)
1637–1638	The Shimabara Rebellion
1639	Policy of *sakoku* introduced (national seclusion); foreigners expelled
1783–1787	The Tenmei famine
1787–1837	Period of Tokugawa Ienari shogunate
1787–1793	Kansei Reforms instituted by Matsudaira Sadanobu
1792	Russian envoy Adam Laxman attempts to visit Japan
1804	Russian envoy Adam Johann von Krusenstern attempts to visit Japan
1806–1807	Russian attacks on disputed, Japanese-held islands in the far north
1808	HMS *Phaeton* Incident, British frigate threatens raid on Nagasaki harbor
1824	British attack southern Japanese island of Takarajima
1825	Japanese shore batteries ordered to fire on all foreign vessels approaching Japan
1833–1836	The Tempō famine
1837	Major riots in Osaka; U.S. merchant ship *Morrison* attempts to visit Japan
1837–1853	Period of Tokugawa Ieyoshi shogunate
1839–1842	Britain defeats China in First Opium War
1841	Tempō reforms instituted by Mizuno Tadakuni

1846	U.S. naval squadron commanded by Commodore James Biddle attempts to visit Japan; French attempt to visit Japan
1849	U.S. naval vessel commanded by Captain James Glynn attempts to visit Japan
1853	Commodore Matthew Perry arrives at the mouth of Edo Bay in command of a squadron of ships, submits letter from President Millard Fillmore to Japanese authorities
1854	Commodore Perry returns and forces the Japanese to sign the Treaty of Kanagawa; Japanese policy of seclusion ended
1854	Great Britain forces Japanese to sign treaty
1855	Russia forces Japanese to sign treaty
1858	France forces Japanese to sign treaty
1858	First U.S. consul, Townsend Harris, negotiates broad commercial and diplomatic treaty between the United States and Japan
1859–1868	Domestic unrest in Japan
1867	Last shogun abdicates, restores power to the emperor
1868	New government formed in Tokyo (formerly Edo); Meiji period begins

CHAPTER ONE
INTRODUCTION

Japan at the Start of Tokugawa Rule

The Battle of Sekigahara, fought in the year 1600, was a pivotal moment in the history of Japan. Tokugawa Ieyasu (1542–1616) and his allies won the battle and ended more than a century of political chaos, intrigue, and civil war. The previous era (known as the Warring States period), which had been characterized by regional warlords exercising authority only in their private domains, gave way to an enduring, semifeudal system under the leadership of the Tokugawa family. Initially, the Tokugawa were understood to be "first among equals" with the other great lords and governed with their assistance in the provinces. But this was a situation the Tokugawa earnestly sought to change. Within two years of Tokugawa Ieyasu becoming shogun in 1603, he abdicated in favor of his son, although he continued to rule behind the scenes until his death in 1616.[1] This political succession solidified the position of the Tokugawa shogun as the supreme leader of Japan. It also created a position that was thereafter filled by a ranking member of the main Tokugawa family line.[2]

As the Tokugawa government took shape in the early seventeenth century, the greatest change to the Japanese political system was that *daimyō* (provincial lords) were required to swear absolute fealty to the Tokugawa

---

1. A shogun was the supreme military dictator of Japan. Warlords could not theoretically confer upon themselves the title of "shogun." This was a position that was given by the emperor. In this case, the Emperor Go-Yōzei (1571–1617) had little choice but to accede to Tokugawa Ieyasu's wishes because he was the single most powerful man in the country.

2. Historians call the years between 1600 and 1868, during which the Tokugawa ruled, the "Tokugawa period." Sometimes it is also called the "Edo period" because the city of Edo was the headquarters of the Tokugawa government.

in Edo.[3] This was a nonnegotiable position. Nonetheless, as long as the *daimyō* kept the peace in their domains (which they ran as personal fiefdoms); provided their allotment of labor to the shogunate; followed the laws and directives issued by the Tokugawa; and, above all, remained loyal to the center, they were allowed to maintain a great deal of control over their lands. This arrangement of fealty and tribute formed the basis of the Baku-Han[4] system of government.

The defining characteristic of the Baku-Han government was authoritarianism on all levels. Only Japanese approved by the authorities were allowed input into any decision-making process. This was as true on the national level as it was on the local. Great lords could not stand in opposition to the Tokugawa any more than peasants could stand in opposition to their local lords. This top-down system did not spring forth from the political settlement immediately following the Battle of Sekigahara, nor was Tokugawa Ieyasu the architect of the entire structure. Rather, the system that was to last until 1868 slowly took its mature form during the reign of the third Tokugawa shogun, Iemitsu (r. 1623–1651), Ieyasu's grandson. For example, the system of alternate attendance (*sankin kōtai*), which required *daimyō* to spend every other year in the city of Edo, was imposed uniformly on all *daimyō* (former foe and ally alike), and "*bukke sho hatto*," the laws and edicts for warriors and warrior houses, were solidified during Iemitsu's rule. Among the many elements of this promulgation was the prohibition of the practice of Christianity (aimed mostly at Roman Catholicism), a proclamation that was a significant cause of the Shimabara Rebellion (1637–1638) in southern Japan. This was a major uprising that posed such an existential threat that the Tokugawa mobilized more than 100,000 samurai to deal with the problem. In the end, nearly 40,000 civilians and rebel samurai were killed.

The Four Classes of Society

Society in Tokugawa Japan was strictly divided into four groups ranked in descending order of importance: samurai, peasants, artisans, and

---

3. At this time, Edo was a small, sleepy fishing village at the head of Tokyo Bay. Edo was later renamed Tokyo.

4. *Baku* is short for *bakufu* (tent government) and *han* is a semiautonomous fiefdom.

merchants. Like many other characteristics of Tokugawa rule, this social structure was an extension and expansion of one of Hideyoshi Toyotomi's policies.[5] The samurai were a military caste whose job was originally to keep the peace. When military threats diminished, and then ceased altogether over several decades in the late seventeenth century, many samurai became government bureaucrats, sometimes abandoning military pursuits but not caste-based prerogatives. As a caste, the samurai represented approximately 7–8 percent of society, a number that increased slightly over time. Peasants and other agricultural workers comprised more than 85 percent of Japanese society in the early seventeenth century. The composition and function of this group changed as the Tokugawa period progressed and more peasants moved into the towns and cities. Skilled laborers, the third class of society, were smithies, carpenters, brewers, potters, and the like. They were valued for their specialized knowledge and for making life more comfortable for all Japanese. Like the peasantry, they were subject to whomever governed the villages or cities in which they lived and worked. The lowest class was the merchants. Conceptually, this system was based on Confucian ideas regarding the natural order of society. Social cohesion and stability were understood to be more important than individual advancement and wealth accumulation. For adherents of Confucianism, merchants contributed little to the betterment of society. As cities grew in the late seventeenth and eighteenth centuries and lasting peace ushered in a long period of prosperity, merchants became wealthy, though not necessarily politically powerful. Sumptuary laws were even passed to restrict outward expressions of wealth. Nonetheless, many wealthy merchants, such as Kinokuniya Bunzaemon (1669–1734), flouted their prosperity and, in so doing, occasionally ran afoul of the authorities.[6] Others, such as Yodoya Tatsugorō (d. 1705), had their fortunes confiscated. Given the visible wealth of many city merchants later in the Tokugawa period, it became difficult to maintain a caste system that was clearly not functioning as effectively as it had in the early years of the seventeenth century.

---

5. Hideyoshi Toyotomi (1537–1598) was the military leader of Japan from 1586 to 1598 and laid the groundwork for many of the systems the Tokugawa rulers later instituted nationwide.

6. Teruoka Yasutaka, "The Pleasure Quarters and Tokugawa Culture," in Andrew Gerstle, ed., *18th Century Japan: Culture and Society* (New York: Routledge Press, 1989), pp. 21–22.

Life for the samurai caste varied greatly according to rank. Some samurai, such as those from great *daimyō* families, were effectively aristocrats. They lived in luxurious homes, had access to the finest clothing and food, achieved high levels of education, had servants to care for their needs, and generally enjoyed a privileged life. However, they did have a responsibility to govern, an often onerous and risky task. On the other end of the spectrum, the lowest samurai foot soldiers (*ashigaru*) lived on a set stipend provided by their lords. They were not allowed to soil their hands with gainful employment and were expected to maintain their martial skills. Given that stipends diminished with the passing generations, lifestyle expectations among low-ranking samurai had to be carefully managed in the second half of the Tokugawa period. Samurai from the middle ranks upward could expect to inherit a stipend (sometimes quite small) and then, if well connected and literate, find employment within the government bureaucracy. No matter their rank or financial position, however, all samurai maintained their privileged position in society.

The Tokugawa system prioritized stability in all things. Peasants, who formed the basis for the system, were theoretically required by law to work the land in perpetuity. Though there was little expectation of social mobility, families sometimes moved up and down on the economic scale within their caste. Small family farms undergirded the economy. Peasants were bound to the land, subject to their lords, and answerable to their village headman. They were, at least in theory, not allowed to leave their villages without the permission of the authorities. Religious pilgrimages offered the only exception to this rule, and the peasantry eagerly embraced any opportunity to visit various shrines and temples.[7]

Most peasants lived predictable lives working the rice paddies and fields; paying taxes (between 40 and 70 percent of that which they produced);[8] marrying and having children; and enjoying the rhythm of the seasons, annual festivals, and the like. In good years, the peasantry enjoyed sufficient food and adequate shelter. In bad years, however, when the peasantry endured poor harvests, natural disasters, or other difficulties, life could be extremely harsh. In the very worst years, peasants starved, sold their children, or committed infanticide when faced with

7. Kenichi Ohno, *The History of Japanese Economic Development: Origins of Private Dynamism* (New York: Routledge Press, 2018), pp. 24–25.

8. Mikiso Hane, *Peasants, Rebels, Women, and Outcastes: The Underside of Modern Japan* (New York: Pantheon, 1982), p. 6.

impossible choices about whom to feed and how to pay their taxes (see Document 2). Rice was the primary staple for those who could afford it. However, most peasants could only eat rice on special occasions. It was simply too expensive to be consumed daily by those who had produced it. There was also a class of landless peasants best described as laborers. Their lives mirrored the lives of laborers in other countries and could be unpredictable, difficult, and short. They worked for prosperous farmers, samurai, and anyone nearby who could pay them. They also endured a high degree of instability based on the labor market.

The Policy of *Sakoku*

During the Warring States period (1477–1600)—that is, the period in Japanese history immediately preceding Tokugawa rule—foreigners had enjoyed nearly unfettered freedom to travel to Japan. Local warlords (*daimyō*) had been more than happy to trade with foreigners, acquire the latest weapons, or learn the newest military tactics from whomever they could. As might be expected given the political chaos of the period, Europeans in Japan during this period also found themselves inexorably drawn into domestic politics. In most cases, Europeans visiting Japan were treated well and found trade and other interactions with Japanese to be quite rewarding (if not under suspicion of working for a rival warlord). But Europeans were a quarrelsome group and sometimes allowed national squabbles back home to play themselves out in Japan. This was, after all, the period of rising tensions just before the European Thirty Years War (1618–1648), a conflict that pitted some of the most prominent Roman Catholic countries against Protestant ones.

Once the Tokugawa gained control of Japan, they wanted to secure its borders and oversee all interactions with foreign nationals (just as contemporary nations seek to monitor and control all who enter and leave). This authoritarian policy mirrored domestic regulations: neither *daimyō* nor peasant could travel freely within Japan. This policy also meant that individual *daimyō* could not enter into agreements with foreign powers because such agreements could potentially threaten the shogunate. However, this policy differed from modern convention by essentially eliminating the free passage of individuals and trade goods between countries. For most of the two centuries the policy was in effect, no Japanese subject could leave Japan at will. Any unfortunate Japanese fisherman shipwrecked in international waters was forced into permanent exile. If they somehow found a way to return, they could be subject to the most serious judicial sanctions. Foreigners were also treated roughly and, as the policy came into effect, expelled from Japan. Later, none were allowed to land without official permission, and until the Russian Laxman Expedition of 1793 (see below), such permission was never granted. Any foreigner caught in Japan illegally was also subject to judicial sanctions. There were exceptions, however. Because the Dutch posed no discernable military threat to the Tokugawa and had provided assistance to the Japanese during the Shimabara Rebellion, they were allowed to maintain a small outpost on an island, known as Dejima, in Nagasaki Bay. Perhaps most importantly to the Japanese, few of the Dutch appeared to be Roman Catholic. On Dejima, the Dutch could engage in strictly limited trade and maintain a modicum of relations between the two countries.[9] However, the Dutch were not allowed on the main islands except during a trip to Edo every other year when they went to pay homage to the shogun. The Koreans and Chinese sent many ships per year to Japan but were confined to Nagasaki and allowed to trade only as specified by the Tokugawa.

The Ryūkyū Kingdom—the group of islands located between Kyushu and Taiwan (now mostly part of the Okinawa archipelago)—was also treated differently. In theory, the Ryūkyū Kingdom was a vassal to Satsuma domain, which invaded and subjugated the islands in 1609. However, the Ryūkyū islanders found themselves in a difficult situation because they were also forced to pay homage (and tribute) to the Ming (and, later, the Qing) Dynasty in China. This unsettled situation lasted until the late nineteenth century when the Qing Dynasty began to collapse.[10] Given that it was not possible to seal off this territory from the

9. Englebert Kaempfer, J. G. Scheuchzer, trans., *The History of Japan: Giving an Account of the Ancient and Present State and Government of That Empire; of Its Temples, Palaces, Castles, and Other Buildings, of Its Metals, Minerals, Trees, Plants, Animals, Birds and Fishes, of the Chronology and Succession of the Emperors, Ecclesiastical and Secular, of the Original Descent, Religions, Customs, and Manufactures of the Natives, and of Their Trade and Commerce with the Dutch and Chinese: Together with a Description of the Kingdom of Siam* (London: Thomas Woodward and Charles Davis, 1728), pp. 364–370.

10. Ronald P. Toby, *State and Diplomacy in Early Modern Japan: Asia in the Development of the Tokugawa Bakufu* (Princeton, NJ: Princeton University Press, 1984), p. 50.

outside world, the Ryūkyū islanders were able to enjoy limited trade and travel. They also became a window into the wider world for the Japanese.[11]

Thus the policy of *sakoku* did not seal off Japan from the rest of humanity. Japan's leaders kept up with the latest global trends, knew of innovative technologies, stayed abreast of current events, and maintained an ever-watchful eye on the Europeans (see Document 12). Japan was not a hermit kingdom, nor did its leadership think itself weak for wanting to control all dealings with the outside world. On the contrary, *sakoku* became a point of pride, an ideological tenet demonstrating the strength and centrality of Japanese civilization.

Japan in the Early Nineteenth Century

Conventional wisdom suggests that life in Japan didn't change much in the two centuries following the founding of the Tokugawa shogunate. However, that would be an incorrect assessment of the country in the early years of the nineteenth century. It is true that many of the structures and institutions put into place by the first three Tokugawa shoguns still existed and largely functioned as they had before. However, Japan was not the same place in the early 1800s as it had been in 1600. Initially, it took many decades for Japan to fully recover from the calamitous conflicts of the Warring States period. But once established, peace, stability, and the imposition of law and order nationwide created conditions for growth in many areas in the seventeenth century. In particular, agriculture flourished, providing a firm foundation for a rapidly growing population. It also laid the groundwork for reliable taxation and a stable government. Examples of development abound, and an assessment of population growth illustrates this phenomenon with clarity. The population of Japan in the year 1600 has been reckoned at less than 10 million. By 1721, the population had risen to 30 million when the first thorough nationwide census was conducted. By 1800, there were perhaps as many as 34 million people in Japan. These numbers indicate that population growth first rose dramatically but then plateaued. This slowdown in growth can be attributed to an economy that stagnated when it reached

11. Kaempfer, *The History of Japan*, pp. 379–381.

a rough equilibrium with the available resources. The slowdown can also be explained by increasing political stasis and changes in agriculture and labor patterns.[12]

Peasants also came to enjoy unexpected agency in the eighteenth and early nineteenth centuries and were able to respond both passively and actively to intolerable living and working conditions, as well as unfair taxation and incompetent governance. Though the country remained agrarian during the Tokugawa period, not all peasants worked the same land the same way, or did the same job their ancestors had. As the period progressed, more and more land accumulated in fewer hands, creating an inequitable system of tenant farming with all its attendant ills. In response, peasants often ran away and moved into the growing villages and towns where they could make a better living. Though such moves were theoretically illegal for most of the Tokugawa period, peasants who moved were often only punished when caught breaking some other law, or during periods of famine or social unrest. The shift in demographics and work patterns often placed a strain on local governments. Only those individuals with families on the official registers of the early Tokugawa years were eligible to become a village headman or community elders. This meant that local government and economic power increasingly resided with an ever-smaller number of landowning gentry. Peasants living illegally as immigrants in a different domain or in a town or city were also theoretically outside the social system. Separated as they were from the land and from the political and social structure, former peasants saw themselves as less-than-willing participants in a system that did not prioritize their needs.[13] There were few official mechanisms for them to make their concerns known or to have them addressed using formal structures. But they were not powerless, and they increasingly made their wishes evident through popular protests known as *ikki*. Ranging in seriousness from local, village-level confrontations between peasants and the authorities, to bloody, regional uprisings in which thousands participated and which required the intervention of the Tokugawa, *ikki* are defined by historians as civil disturbances of any size. In the seventeenth century, the total number of *ikki* recorded nationwide was 420. The total number

12. Akira Hayami, *Population, Family and Society in Pre-Modern Japan* (Folkstone, UK: Brill/Global Oriental Press, 2010), pp. 92–93, 96.

13. Thomas C. Smith, *The Agrarian Origins of Modern Japan* (Palo Alto, CA: Stanford University, 1959), pp. 183–185.

of *ikki* recorded nationwide in the eighteenth century was 1,092. As the political situation deteriorated between 1800 and 1867, there were 1,188 recorded *ikki*—and they increased in severity in the later years.[14] In a particularly telling example, an *ikki* involving more than 200,000 peasants erupted in the Kanto area (around present-day Tokyo) in 1764.[15] These public outbursts occurred for different reasons in different areas of Japan and were initiated by different groups of people. However, many *ikki* were well planned and executed for greatest effect. Examined as a group, these statistics indicate a general restiveness among the peasantry, an unwillingness to remain subordinate, and a certain degree of fearlessness about the most serious judicial sanctions being imposed upon them.

Samurai living patterns also changed in the eighteenth and nineteenth centuries. In the seventeenth century, samurai largely lived in or near the castles of their lords and away from the major cities. The lord of a fiefdom extracted taxes, money, services, and goods (mostly in the form of rice) from the peasantry. These tributes were then distributed to the local samurai who administered the domains. During this earlier period, samurai were understood to be warrior-protectors working in the interests of each domain. But in the eighteenth century, the samurai—like many peasants—also moved into the growing cities and away from castle towns and garrisons. This had several unintended consequences. In addition to separating them from the land and the population they administered, it also changed the perception of the samurai among the population. Samurai increasingly became hereditary bureaucrats, faceless functionaries who were paid an ever-diminishing stipend. Many samurai endured humiliation as they slowly became impoverished and/or indebted to local merchants (see Document 1). In the cities it was more difficult to maintain their training and martial skills. The warrior caste was therefore slowly transformed into a privileged class without assuming many of the risks associated with their status. This was also at odds with the Confucian ethic that undergirded the social structure of the era. In this ethos, promotions were earned through meritorious conduct and not awarded based solely on family or connections. Warriors in previous epochs had been able to distinguish themselves on the battlefield—a sort

---

14. Stephen Vlastos, *Peasant Protest and Uprisings in Tokugawa Japan* (Berkeley: University of California Press, 1990), p. 75.

15. Hane, *Peasants, Rebels, Women, and Outcastes*, p. 7.

of merit. But in the long period of peace, it became much more difficult for hereditary bureaucrats to do the same.[16]

As has been noted above, peasants increasingly moved into towns and cities over the course of the eighteenth and nineteenth centuries. Since there was an acute shortage of fields in densely populated urban spaces, what were those former farmers doing? The answer is complicated, variable according to location, and largely based on economics. In the Tokugawa system, peasants were supposed to work the land full time and provide the nourishment needed to sustain the population. However, in the eighteenth and nineteenth centuries, peasants increasingly spent more time engaged in pursuits that were only indirectly associated with farming. These were known as "by-employments." Among the many pursuits included in this category were the processing of cotton (ginning and spinning), sericulture (silk production), ceramics, paper production, ironworking, and the like. Thomas Smith, the eminent agricultural historian of Japan, has argued that in some areas peasants derived more than 50 percent of their income from nonfarming pursuits in the late Tokugawa period.[17] (The government also did not initially have a thorough system of taxation on these products.) When the time came to move off the farmsteads, these skills were easily transferable to towns and cities. Growing urban markets for these products added to the allure of city life. Good roads and bridges were required to move these products, as well as inns and portage services—and an entire transportation infrastructure grew to meet the demand.[18] The fact that these peasants were still able to feed the population while devoting a significant portion of their time to by-employments indicates that advances in farming techniques provided farmers with ample free time. However, this situation also led to little increase in overall yield and provided little margin in time of drought, flood, or other natural disasters.

Because Japan transitioned so quickly to the industrial age in the late nineteenth century, economic historians have long argued about the extent to which there were early indications of industrialization in the late Tokugawa period before Westerners arrived. The system of part-time farming and part-time by-employments enjoyed by the peasants

---

16. Thomas C. Smith, *Native Sources of Japanese Industrialization, 1750–1920* (Berkeley: University of California Press, 1989), pp. 10–11.

17. Smith, *Native Sources of Japanese Industrialization*, pp. 78–79.

18. Kaempfer, *The History of Japan*, pp. 344–345.

allowed for a critical mass of workers to develop skills that were easily adaptable to the industrial age. Indeed, many were already working with iron and other metals. Almost as important, there was an existing commercial environment and a workforce with basic literacy and mathematical skills, a sophisticated infrastructure that included a well-developed transportation and communication network, and accumulated capital among the merchants in the cities.

Economic and Political History in the Early Nineteenth Century

By the late eighteenth and early nineteenth centuries, the Tokugawa rulers had lost the vision and resourcefulness that characterized many of their predecessors' rules. Gone were the great men who, while protecting the prerogatives of the ruling class, also considered the best interests of the country when making decisions. At exactly the time when careful, incisive leadership was called for, Japan was saddled instead with a series of shoguns less interested in good governance than in their harems and outrageous displays of excess. Indeed, the eleventh shogun, Tokugawa Ienari (r. 1787–1837), is remembered as perhaps the most thoroughly debauched shogun in Japanese history. It was not always so with Ienari, initially known as a reformer who tackled the worst excesses of the period by rooting out corruption, excessive government spending, and peasant absconsion.[19]

In the years leading up to Ienari's rule, the Tenmei famine (1783–1787) gripped the land and resulted in the deaths of at least 1 million of the 34 million inhabitants of Japan. The Tokugawa leadership believed, among other things, that the famine was partially the result of peasants abandoning the land and moving to other areas. Historians now believe that the large number of vagrant peasants was the *consequence*, not cause, of the famine. For example, one day in 1786, in Tosa domain on the island of Shikoku, the *daimyō* Yamauchi Genzō, out on a hunting

19. This is legal term that described the situation when a peasant (or samurai), who was bound to the land by law, ran away without permission. This deprived the lord or landowner of labor, income, and produce. Absconsion was illegal in Japan during the Tokugawa period. It should be noted, however, that peasants in Japan were not slaves or serfs, but they still lacked freedom of movement.

expedition, was surprised to encounter a large number of angry peasants who had the gall to confront him about the privations they faced. He heard them out and left quickly. Nonetheless, the peasants soon thereafter burned the home of one of his most hated officials—the man whom the peasants blamed for their suffering. At least 700 of the peasants then fled to a neighboring domain and begged to be allowed to stay.[20] Partially in response to the many food-related riots in the country (including large riots in Osaka and Edo), Ienari appointed his kinsman Matsudaira Sadanobu (1759–1829) to the position of head councilor.[21]

Once in office, Sadanobu instituted what came to be known as the Kansei Reforms (1787–1793). These reforms were designed to address problems associated with the Tenmei famine and its accompanying ills. Sadanobu is remembered as a pragmatic reformer, but also a moralist and social conservative. Thus, he characterized many of the problems in the country as ethical failings and directed many of his reforms to address these weaknesses. He identified three problems: the shortage of goods and services in Edo (and by extension, other big cities), inflation, and excessive consumption. For much of the early Edo period, the samurai sought to maintain thorough control over the lives of all commoners. This included what they ate, how long they worked, what crops they planted, how they dressed, how they lived, and so on. So it came as no surprise that the Kansei Reforms included a forced return to austerity and abstemiousness among 90+ percent of the population. Of course, peasants, merchants, and artisans alike did not see the problem in the same way as Sadanobu, and they did their best to passively resist or ignore many of his dictates, including those concerning price controls, sumptuary laws, and social restrictions. In an example related to the Tosa domain protests of the previous year, a district official not associated with the protests wrote:

> After the peasants of Ikegawa village fled the domain last year, the hearts of the people did not rest, and they did not listen to the directives of the government. When the county magistrate proceeded through the land and gathered village headmen, village elders, and group leaders, etc., to a reading

20. Luke S. Roberts, "A Petition for a Popularly Chosen Council of Government in Tosa in 1787," *Harvard Journal of Asiatic Studies* 57, no. 2 (December 1997): 583–584.

21. Daniel V. Botsman, *Punishment and Power in the Making of Modern Japan* (Princeton, NJ: Princeton University Press, 2007), pp. 104–105.

> of the laws and proclamations, the headmen and elders were respectful, but the group leaders and all below could not have cared in the least. They yawned and slept in a completely unlawful manner and, on their way home, made all sorts of jokes and insults. They said things like, "I went to a ballad performance today, but the chanter was so poor we were all bored to death!" Or they reviled the reader: "He stopped and started and was most boring. He certainly needs more practice." They did not have the slightest fear of their superiors. I heard the people saying, "As strange as the world is today whatever we say to the rulers is of no use. The only thing to know is that it is most important to look out for oneself." This was unbearably alarming. The thing that worried me most was that perhaps the annual rent would not come in smoothly. I was so distressed I could not happily eat or sleep.[22]

It is clear that the peasants were not concerned about the potential repercussions of their actions and were contemptuous of the government. It is also clear that Tokugawa officials were only interested in what could be extracted from the peasantry. The fabric of the social contract had begun to fray.

The Kansei Reforms also addressed overspending by the government and general profligacy by the samurai caste (see Document 6). These financial reforms eventually hit the shogun's pocketbook and affected his lifestyle, forcing Sadanobu's resignation and the eventual abandonment of the reforms. We can say, then, that the Kansei Reforms failed.[23] Soon thereafter, the food shortages subsided as the agricultural sector recovered from the natural disasters that had actually caused much of the famine in the first place. From 1804 to 1830, Japan enjoyed a period of plenty during which time Ienari's profligate spending continued and his general disinterest in governing was camouflaged. The failed Kansei Reforms served to demonstrate the extent to which the population was able to ignore an increasingly feckless government, one that also risked growing unpopular with many *daimyō*.

---

22. Roberts, "A Petition for a Popularly Chosen Council of Government in Tosa," 583–584.

23. Isao Soranaka, "The Kansei Reforms—Success or Failure," *Monumenta Nipponica* 33, no. 2 (Summer 1978): 151–164.

A second major famine occurred during the reign of Tokugawa Ienari, this time late in his life. This event, more than just about any other domestic problem, clearly illustrated the general weakness of the government. The Tempō famine lasted from 1833 to 1836 and was more widespread than the Kansei famine. This famine occurred because of very cold temperatures and wild variations in rainfall—first too little, and then too much. Though such natural disasters were uncommon, the government had certainly responded effectively to similar events in the past. When, in the first half of the Tokugawa period, a year of poor harvests led to starvation among the peasantry, the authorities had opened the government's stores of emergency grain and helped alleviate the worst misery. Yet, the Tempō period government seemed incapable of acting in a meaningful way. At the same time, tax revenues were at their lowest in 125 years, putting additional stress on the government. At the height of the famine, the ruling elites were unable to maintain public order. Just trying to survive, many commoners wandered the countryside in search of food, joined gangs, or engaged in petty theft. Some situations were truly pitiful. In Osaka, an average of thirty–forty people starved to death per day and infants were abandoned.[24] In Kaga domain on the Sea of Japan, conditions in one village became desperate. An official conveyed the following observation:

> There is no end to the dying. . . . The corpses are piled into huge pits at Kasamae Village. . . . The stench is overwhelming, and large dogs come out at night and gnaw on the bones of the dead. We have stationed Foot Soldiers there for three days and three nights to shoot them with guns.[25]

There were 445 known *ikki* (and other urban riots) during this period, indicating widespread disorder. It was, of course, not unknown for peasants and townspeople to become restive in the Tokugawa period. But it was the scale of the Tempō famine and the scope of the resulting public disorder that were unprecedented.[26]

---

24. John H. Miller, "Social Disorder in Late Tokugawa Japan" (unpublished PhD diss., Princeton University, 1975), pp. 179–183.

25. James L. McClain, "Failed Expectations: Kaga Domain on the Eve of the Meiji Restoration," *The Journal of Japanese Studies* 14, no. 2 (Summer 1988): 412.

26. William B. Hauser, *Economic Institutional Change in Tokugawa Japan: Osaka and the Kinai Cotton Trade* (Cambridge: Cambridge University Press, 1974), pp. 53–57.

Ienari named a new chief councilor, Mizuno Tadakuni (1794–1851), and tasked him with addressing these mounting disasters. Tadakuni took the same sorts of actions that Sadanobu, his predecessor, had: he implemented sumptuary laws, demanded a return to austerity and hard work, sought to regain control over spending, reduced prices and wages by 20 percent (in Edo and Osaka), tried to send peasants back to their ruined farms, restricted theater attendance, and the like. Tadakuni was also forced to deal with the many *daimyō* who were becoming openly recalcitrant and exasperated with Tokugawa leadership. In an effort to regain some control over commerce, he reformed a number of village and city markets, undertook limited land transfers, and even revoked some *daimyō* monopolies. But his actions had unintended consequences. For example, Tadakuni forgave many samurai debts—just as the government had done during the Kansei Reforms. This time, however, many of the merchants left holding unpaid loans were ruined and those who stayed afloat refused (to the extent possible) to make further loans. The samurai were later galled to discover that they would have to pay higher rates for loans or simply do without.[27] To make matters worse, some samurai were not being paid their stipend. In Kaga domain, for example, the *daimyō* refused to pay his samurai retainers, calling their salaries "loans."[28] As might be expected, the Tempō Reforms (1841–1843) were extremely unpopular among most of the population. And Tadakuni remained unsuccessful in his attempts to address the underlying causes of economic distress.

The Kansei and Tempō famines and subsequent reforms showed that the Tokugawa were incapable of responding effectively to an economic crisis—or worse, that the system and government were rotten all the way to the core. There was a palpable sense that something was not right and the people were increasingly unwilling to remain quiet. A well-known illustration of this problem was the failed revolt of Osaka official Ōshio Heihachirō (1793–1837) in 1837. Ōshio was a Confucian scholar, samurai, and police magistrate who, during the worst of the famine, sold his possessions to alleviate the suffering of the starving and destitute. In the early weeks of the crisis, he had pleaded with government officials for relief and assistance. After receiving no meaningful response, he called

27. Hauser, *Economic Institutional Change in Tokugawa Japan*, pp. 53–57.

28. E. Sydney Crawcour, "Economic Change in the Nineteenth Century," in Kozo Yamamura, ed., *The Economic Emergence of Modern Japan*, Vol. 1 (New York: Cambridge University Press, 1997), p. 26.

for a general uprising. The rebellion caused widespread destruction despite the government's attempts to suppress it by force. At least 18,000 structures burned to the ground in Osaka. Still, the insurrection did not spread beyond the region. After penning a memorial that characterized Tokugawa officials as corrupt and unresponsive, Ōshio committed suicide and became a martyr (see Document 3). To be sure, there were other protest movements during the first half of the nineteenth century. But this one resonated in Japan and many protesters later drew inspiration and guidance from Ōshio's writings.

Though in 1837 Ienari technically abdicated in favor of his son Ieyoshi (r. 1837–1853), who was shogun when Commodore Perry first visited, Ienari continued to wield informal power until his death in 1841. Tadakuni continued as chief councilor until he was exiled in 1845. By this point, it was clear that meaningful reform on the national level was likely not going to succeed. However, given the semifeudal structure of the Tokugawa system, it was possible for individual *daimyō* to undertake reform in their own domains. These attempts at reform yielded decidedly mixed results depending on the domain.

In the decade before the Tempō reforms, several *daimyō* successfully instituted moderate reforms in their domains. Initiated without any national coordination, these reforms addressed only local concerns. Chōshū domain, in particular, began a series of reforms to address its 80,000 *kan* (copper coin) debt, an amount that, in the 1840s, represented approximately 84 percent of its annual economic output.[29] This debt weighed heavily on the minds of their *daimyō* and was known by Chōshū Minister of Reform Murata Seifū (1783–1855) as the "80,000 *kan* enemy."[30] A return to parsimony, thrift, and abnegation in the region allowed domainal authorities to maintain this significant debt at a manageable level. Many other domains unsuccessfully attempted similar actions. Strengthened, in part, by these stabilizing reforms, Chōshū domain was able to effectively oppose the Tokugawa authorities in the 1850s and 1860s.

Other domains, such as Satsuma, found ways to manage their debt load and attempted political reforms as well. Most political reforms were minor and did not result in large-scale reorganization or the removal

29. Shunsaku Nishikawa, "The Economy of Chōshū on the Eve of Industrialization," *The Economic Studies Quarterly* 38, no. 4 (December 1987): 324–325.

30. Albert M. Craig, *Chōshū in the Meiji Restoration* (Cambridge, MA: Harvard University Press, 1967), pp. 54–55.

of officials at the domain level. Rather, *daimyō* attempted to address some of the worst situations by providing outlets for grievances. Tosa, another domain that ultimately found a way to successfully oppose the Tokugawa, achieved this by creating petition boxes into which commoners could drop notes about corrupt officials or make suggestions for reform. These suggestions were, according to the historian Luke Roberts, rarely implemented. However, they did allow Tosa officials to more accurately gauge just how unhappy or disgruntled the peasantry had become. In this, an era of peasant protest, it was crucial that the government understand the level of dissatisfaction among the people.[31]

Gunboat Diplomacy and Western Imperialism

In the late eighteenth century, a new force—industrialization—was shaking up world politics. During this period, smaller, seafaring countries started the process of industrialization and slowly began to enjoy outsized economic and military influence. This challenged the old order when massive, land-based empires dominated their regions as undisputed hegemons. For example, the Mughal Empire in India and the Qing Empire in China had been among the strongest and wealthiest in world history in the early eighteenth century. Indeed, Chinese Emperor Qianlong (r. 1735–1796) ruled a nation with a population of 300 million, nearly two times greater than any other, and controlled territory significantly larger than even contemporary China. It was also largely self-sufficient as an economic unit, highly advanced technologically, and politically stable. In short, it compared favorably to the combined strength of all the countries of western and central Europe at the same time. Nonetheless, the Mughal and Qing Empires were already in decline and not in a position to meet the new challenge of industrialization when the smaller nations of Europe began to make demands of them in the late eighteenth century. But India and China were well acquainted with imperialism and had practiced it, in one form or another, for thousands of years. China, in particular, was unwilling to allow the upstart Europeans to trade or establish diplomatic relations outside of the existing system of vassalage. The Europeans had been powerless to change

31. Roberts, "A Petition for a Popularly Chosen Council of Government in Tosa," 575–596.

the situation until the industrial revolution shifted the balance of power in their direction.

The combination of rapid industrialization in Great Britain and the precipitous decline of the Qing Empire allowed for the rise of "gunboat diplomacy" in East Asia. Relatively small advances in science and technology led to the creation of stronger metals and the harnessing of steam for the purposes of propulsion. Steam engines mounted on ships could drive paddle wheels and propellers, giving commanders the ability to go when and where they wanted regardless of wind direction and sometimes at speeds greater than were possible with sail. Shipboard cannon made of stronger metals could accept more gunpowder, leading to greater range. The new British ships traversed coastal regions, traveled up river estuaries, and steamed into harbors to bombard defenses and did so with impunity because they could quickly outmaneuver land-based artillery. If necessary, commanders could temporarily land a small number of soldiers—equipped with modern firearms—to attack, plunder, and pillage unsuspecting villages and cities and then leave before an effective local response could be mustered. These minor skirmishes could not and did not cause the collapse of the Chinese diplomatic order in East Asia, but by taking advantage of existing domestic weaknesses in China, they revealed to already restive populations in China (and elsewhere in East Asia) just how ineffective the Chinese government had become and how far behind they were militarily.

Over several decades in the late eighteenth and early nineteenth centuries, Great Britain and Russia were able to continuously harass, with increasing fearlessness, less developed countries all over the world. The Westerners created such instability in these realms that most countries succumbed to the pressure of gunboat diplomacy and signed unequal treaties. If weaker countries refused, many were subjugated outright. Yet East Asia posed a number of unique problems for the European imperialists. Most of the countries bordering China were titular vassal states, and any European attempt to interfere with those countries risked intervention by the Chinese. British attempts with the Macartney (1793) and Amherst (1816) Embassies to the Qing court yielded no normalization of commercial and diplomatic ties. This frustrated British designs in East Asia. And so it was that the Europeans mostly played by Chinese rules in East Asia until the First Opium War (1839–1842). During that war, the British used their navy to great effect by attacking various Chinese forts, blockading ports, and generally harassing the coast until the Qing sued for peace. It should be made clear that Britain could in no way have invaded, conquered, and occupied China, even after the First Opium War. But the situation frustrated the Qing to such an extent that they were willing to pay the British to—as the Chinese understood it—quit fighting and go away.

Initially, China had little intention of upholding their end of the Treaty of Nanjing (1842), which brought an end to the First Opium War. Among the most objectionable terms of the Treaty was the requirement that they had to open several treaty ports to the British and allow long-term residence of some foreign nationals. Such terms were shocking to the Chinese and in strict contravention of their diplomatic norms. Soon thereafter, France also signed a treaty with China and the European scramble for Chinese concessions was on. The Chinese system of vassalage and influence in foreign affairs—which had largely prevented broader foreign interference in the region—collapsed within a generation as China, struggling with its own problems, could not successfully come to the aid of any of its vassal states. East Asia was suddenly open to the predacious European imperialists.

The Japanese policy of seclusion (*sakoku*), which placed strict controls on all foreign interaction with Japan, had been created using the Chinese example. It shocked the Japanese to discover that China was unable to maintain its diplomatic system.[32] Japan had not, strictly speaking, been a part of the Chinese system of vassalage. They had participated on very rare occasions over the centuries when it suited them. But more often, Japan didn't recognize Chinese diplomatic norms. Nonetheless, the Japanese accepted that China was the superpower of East Asia. If they wanted to respond effectively to the threat posed by Europe and the United States, the Japanese knew that they would have to be nimbler and cleverer, diplomatically speaking, than the Chinese had been.

Early European Efforts to Establish Diplomatic Relations with Japan

The late eighteenth and early nineteenth centuries saw a number of failed European attempts to establish commercial and diplomatic ties with

32. Tashiro Kazui and Susan Downing Videen, "Foreign Relations During the Edo Period: Sakoku Reexamined," *Journal of Japanese Studies* 8, no. 2 (1982): 288.

Japan. But as European weapons became increasingly sophisticated and powerful—and as they were thus able to put more muscle behind their gunboat diplomacy—the Westerners put more pressure on the Japanese. One of the first European attempts to make contact with the Japanese occurred in 1792, when the Russian envoy Adam Laxman (1766–1806) sought to return shipwrecked Japanese sailors to the northern island of Hokkaidō. Laxman's mission provided a pretext to visit Edo and hold talks with Tokugawa officials. However, after a series of negotiations with the Japanese *daimyō* in Hokkaidō (a frontier region at the time) failed, and word came from Edo that he could not visit, Laxman was given permission to land one Russian ship at Nagasaki. He was then instructed to petition the shogun through the usual channels. Instead, believing himself to be a failure, he returned to Russia. Undeterred by the failure of this initial mission, Tsar Alexander I (1777–1825) sent Adam Johann von Krusenstern to try again. Before leaving on this 1804–1805 expedition, von Krusenstern (1770–1846) was appointed to be ambassador to Japan—and he carried with him Laxman's permission to land at Nagasaki. Much to his consternation, von Krusenstern was denied by the Japanese, but at least he was allowed to depart in peace. The Russians then engaged in a series of attacks on the Sakhalin and Kurile Islands in 1806 and 1807. Though it was not entirely clear which country owned Sakhalin, the Japanese did assert ownership of the Kuriles and understood the Russian action to be an attack on their interests. Subsequent Russian incursions in 1811–1813 alarmed the Japanese but did not result in any substantial changes aside from the strengthening of some coastal defenses. Though it continued to keep foreigners at bay, Japan's policy of *sakoku* was being probed for weaknesses.

To the Japanese, the 1808 *Phaeton* Incident was one of the most disturbing episodes of the early nineteenth century. The *Phaeton,* a British frigate, was patrolling the Indian and Pacific Oceans during the Napoleonic campaigns. When the Dutch succumbed to the French, the British navy targeted their ships. Flying the colors of a captured Dutch flag, the *Phaeton* sailed into Nagasaki Harbor looking for Dutch ships. Upon realizing there were no Dutch ships to be attacked, the British sailors demanded that the Japanese provide them with supplies. Before the Japanese or Dutch representatives living in Nagasaki knew what had happened, the British had taken several Dutchmen hostage. The British then threatened to kill the Dutch hostages and sink the other ships in the harbor if not provided with the items they sought. After a brief show of force, the Japanese realized their shore batteries could not fire effectively on the British vessel and gave in to British demands—and the *Phaeton* sailed away. The Japanese leadership believed this incident to be a failure, albeit an isolated one. Various punishments were handed out and at least one commander committed suicide. Harbor defenses were beefed up and some military reforms initiated, but the greater threat posed by the Westerners went unrecognized.

The British again violated Japanese seclusion in 1818, landing sailors near Edo and generally causing trouble. Unable, during that trip, to convince the Tokugawa authorities to reconsider their policy of *sakoku,* the British returned in 1824. This time, violence broke out when the British landed a small group on the southern island of Takarajima. Buildings were destroyed and at least one British sailor was killed. This clash led to the first significant change of Japanese policy in several decades—though it was not the change the British sought. In 1825, the shogun ordered Japanese commanders to fire upon and sink all foreign vessels not preapproved for a visit. Any foreigners who managed to land were to be arrested—and executed if they resisted. As the Tokugawa authorities did not strictly enforce this edict, however, it sounded more impressive than it actually was. When in 1837 the *Morrison,* an American vessel, attempted to land at two different Japanese ports, it was fired upon but was not vigorously pursued. Rather than carry out their order, the Japanese authorities directly contravened the 1825 edict. Far from immediately destroying the vessel, the authorities provided them with supplies and politely asked them to leave.

The Chinese defeat in the First Opium War and the subsequent imposition of the Treaty of Nanjing should have caused the Tokugawa leadership to dramatically alter its position on the policy of *sakoku.* Mizuno Tadakuni and other leaders were well aware that continued seclusion was a risky policy. There were high-level consultations in Edo and shore defenses were enhanced yet again in preparation for the appearance of the Westerners. In 1842, the Tokugawa authorities relaxed their 1825 edict just a little: they would provide basic supplies to distressed foreign ships. But serious proposals to abandon the policy of *sakoku* never resulted in substantial change. Even after the king of Holland, Willem II (1792–1849), sent a letter in 1844 advising that the Tokugawa authorities modify the policy or risk serious hostilities with the British, there was no change. The policy seemed to be sacrosanct.

CHAPTER TWO THE WESTERN NATIONS ATTEMPT TO VISIT JAPAN

International diplomacy is fraught with peril. Miscommunication, misunderstanding, and missed signals are often the rule and not the exception. However, in the case of Japan in the middle decades of the nineteenth century, the demands of all sides were generally well understood. As explained in the previous chapter, the Japanese government wanted to control its borders and maintain its seclusion. But its government was increasingly ineffectual, its leaders conflicted, and its future very much in doubt. At the same time, several nations wanted Japan to enter into the global community but only under conditions defined by the Western imperial powers. Perhaps most importantly, those Western powers were willing to use force to get what they wanted, as they had done in numerous other countries. Many Western rulers and intellectuals were convinced of their cultural superiority and adhered strongly to the concept of the "White man's burden" popularized by British author Rudyard Kipling (1865–1936) in his poem of the same name: the idea that white Europeans had a moral obligation to bring "civilization" to nonwhite peoples. Thus, the Western imperialists believed firmly, but incorrectly, that they were bringing to Japan the blessings of Western civilization. After all, Western imperialists took it as an article of faith that the combination of "commerce, knowledge, and Christianity, with their multiplied blessings" would be good for Japan.[1] Their attitude was paternalistic and condescending and it appeared that Japan would be forced to embrace Western ideals and international structures whether or not the Japanese liked it.

The forced "opening" of Japan was a complicated process, and the events that led to it unfolded in an unpredictable fashion. Several of the Western nations involved were also rivals and competed with each other to expand their empires in East Asia. Each of these Western nations was looking to establish new markets for their manufactured goods, to expand

1. H. Blodget, "A Sketch of the Life and Services of the Late S. W. Williams, LLD," *The Chinese Recorder and Missionary Journal* XV (May–June 1884): 217.

trade, and to acquire new possessions—and, if possible, to prevent their rivals from establishing new colonial possessions. They therefore carefully monitored each other as they plotted their next moves. Russia (in earlier decades), France, Great Britain, and the United States all wanted to "open" Japan, and only the first nation to succeed in doing so would enjoy the enhanced prestige and the fruits of their labor.

France

The French were late entering the Pacific basin. They had not been particularly active there in the seventeenth and eighteenth centuries, and the Napoleonic wars kept them otherwise occupied during the early nineteenth century. Starting in the 1840s, however, they intended to make up for lost time. In 1844, the French landed a corvette, the *Alcmène*, at Naha (the capital of the Ryūkyū Kingdom) with two missionaries, orders to negotiate a commercial agreement, and a desire to lay the groundwork for a later visit by Admiral Jean-Baptiste Cécille (1787–1873).[2] The missionaries were allowed to stay for a few years, but the French otherwise made little headway. Nonetheless, Admiral Cécille arrived, uninvited, at Naha in 1846 and suggested that the only way to keep the British from seizing the islands was to make them a French protectorate. Unmoved but greatly alarmed, the Ryūkyū authorities sent word, via Satsuma domain, to the Tokugawa authorities in Edo. Edo delegated authority back to Satsuma, which then steadfastly refused any accommodation with the French. After failing in the Ryūkyūs, Admiral Cécille immediately sailed to Nagasaki with three warships to engage in direct negotiations with Tokugawa representatives. He was again rebuffed and the French squadron sailed away. According to historian Meron Medzini, the French government determined that it would have to significantly reposition its resources to use force effectively and, given that Japan was not its highest priority in East Asia, determined that the prize did not merit the effort or the risk.[3]

---

2. Admiral Cécille was also known for bombarding the Vietnamese port of Danang and sinking several Vietnamese vessels—all of which facilitated the growing French presence in Southeast Asia.

3. Meron Medzini, *French Policy in Japan during the Closing Years of the Tokugawa Regime* (Cambridge, MA: East Asian Research Center, Harvard University, 1971), pp. 3–7.

Great Britain

As the world's strongest naval power, Great Britain posed the greatest threat to Japan. Since the end of the First Opium War, the British had plotted to find an easy way to open Japan and impose upon that country a treaty similar to the one they imposed on China. The Foreign Office had to walk a fine line, however, because the British public was more than a little queasy about its government's role promoting opium in China and had little appetite for additional large-scale violence in yet another country, all in the pursuit of profits. In addition, rumbles were beginning to be heard in Parliament about the cost to British taxpayers of administering some of the larger, more unruly colonies such as India. Indeed, there were so many untapped markets and commercial opportunities in China alone that it would take decades to even determine what was already available. For Britain, Japan was simply not as big a prize as China and there was little perceived need to precipitate a crisis with the island country. Therefore, British actions with regard to Japan were circumspect, almost careful, when compared to its actions in China. That said, the British were ever the opportunists and keen not to be the last in on the latest action.

For Britain and other nations, Japan itself and, more specifically, access to Japanese markets, were not necessarily the prize. Instead, many of the islands claimed by Japan near the Ryūkyū Kingdom were considered important as a potential safe harbor from which one might continue to exploit China if security conditions deteriorated on the mainland. It is important to remember that in the 1840s and 1850s, it was far from certain that China would not quickly recover from the losses it endured in the First Opium War and rise once again to threaten British interests in East Asia. Britain's military position in China in the first decade after the war was extremely tenuous: one wrong move risked expulsion or the start of an unwinnable war. On the other hand, many Japanese islands boasted deepwater ports, ample coal, and plentiful supplies of food and water. All that was needed was Japanese government cooperation, which was not forthcoming. The British had followed closely French Admiral Cécille's unsuccessful efforts in Nagasaki and, in light of continued Japanese inflexibility, determined in 1846 to postpone sending a squadron to Japan until they could bring sufficient force to bear or until conditions required they act. Although a small number of British merchants and missionaries petitioned the government to make Japan a priority and even landed unwelcome guests in the Ryūkyū Islands on two occasions, the British Foreign Office didn't shift its position. This was in part because the British became aware of concrete plans by the United States.

The United States

The United States became a continental power with astonishing speed in the 1840s. In the Oregon Treaty of 1846, Great Britain ceded to the United States formal control of what are today the states of Oregon and Washington. This ended a long-standing disagreement about which nation would exercise jurisdiction over the territory. In addition, the Mexican-American War (1846–1848) freed U.S. settlers to turn California into a territory in 1848 and then a state in 1850. Settlers poured in and gold was discovered, speeding the displacement of the Native American population and the exploitation of the land. With the Pacific fully accessible, the United States had to quickly reorient its policies regarding the countries on the Pacific Rim. By this point in history, the United States had developed crucial, long-term interests in the region in ways that it had not just a decade before. Commerce, diplomacy, and other matters of state were just a few of the many issues requiring discussion with Japan. It is therefore easy to divine the intentions of the U.S. government in the late 1840s and early 1850s as it sought to find ways to effectuate change to the Japanese policy of seclusion.

Japan was sending mixed messages during this time. The United States government was well aware that seclusion was the foundation of all Japanese foreign policy. No fewer than twenty-seven U.S. commercial and military vessels had attempted to visit Japan between the founding of the republic and 1853.[4] U.S. policy makers had carefully followed British, French, and earlier Russian (see Document 4) attempts as those countries tried in vain to open dialogue with the Japanese. The United States also knew that the Russian Empire intended to try its luck again as soon as possible. Well aware of the fact that in 1825 the Japanese government had hardened its position on repelling foreign visitors, the U.S. government puzzled over Japan's apparent softening of that rule in 1842, following China's defeat in the First Opium War. The only way to be sure

4. Amy S. Greenberg, *Manifest Manhood and the Antebellum American Empire* (Cambridge: Cambridge University Press, 2005), p. 261.

of the Japanese policy regarding foreign visitors was to ask them about it directly—but it would have been a mistake to accept any answer as definitive, given the factional infighting in the Tokugawa government and the fact that any individual *daimyō* might simply ignore the directives of the central Tokugawa rulers.

The United States had long wanted to force Japan to treat U.S. sailors decently, providing them with aid and shelter when shipwrecked or in distress. Indeed, it was at the time customary practice for all seafaring peoples to safeguard the lives of all castaways (except during wartime). The sheer number of American sailors involved in the whaling industry—along with the explosion of commerce between China and the United States following the First Opium War—made this an especially urgent issue for the U.S. government.

With newly expanded access to the Pacific, and with a merchant fleet quickly transitioning to steam propulsion, American merchants wanted to extend their reach in the East. But extended steam travel required greater access to the coal that powered the ships, and merchants were reluctant to devote valuable cargo space to hauling that extra fuel. Japan suddenly seemed like a very convenient place for U.S. steamships to stop, refuel, and reprovision.

Two incidents serve to illustrate the Tokugawa government's mixed messages regarding the return of shipwrecked sailors. In 1837, the U.S. merchant vessel *Morrison* set sail with the stated intention of returning seven Japanese shipwrecked sailors. As with the earlier Russian attempts in Hokkaidō, however, this rescue mission was merely a pretext to land and initiate talks regarding the possibility of commercial interaction. The *Morrison* did not receive the warm welcome it was seeking. Japanese shore batteries fired at the *Morrison* on sight and drove it out of Edo Bay. The ship was then fired upon a second time as it attempted to land at Kagoshima. The *Morrison* left without provisions and without having returned the forlorn Japanese sailors to their homeland. Yet when it could be reasonably sure of motive, the Japanese government sometimes agreed to receive ships returning shipwrecked Japanese sailors. In 1843, the U.S. whaling vessel *Manhattan* returned twenty-two Japanese sailors who had been stranded when their ship foundered near the Bonin Islands. Having granted the *Manhattan* permission to land in Edo Bay, the Japanese provided the ship with supplies of food and water, refusing any payment. For the first time in centuries, a Western vessel obtained official permission to land someplace other than

Nagasaki—an important development. Yet the captain of the *Manhattan* was warned never to return to Japan.

In 1846, President James K. Polk (1795–1849), an ardent promoter of U.S. expansion, sent Commodore James Biddle (1783–1848) to Japan with instructions to gently inquire about the possibility of talks. Commanding two naval vessels, the *Columbus* and the *Vincennes*, Biddle sailed into Edo Bay and forwarded a message to the shogun. It reads:

> I send you, by this letter, an envoy of my own appointment, an officer of high rank in his country, who is no missionary of religion. He goes by my command to bear you my greeting and good wishes, and to promote friendship and commerce between the two countries.
>
> You know that the United States of America now extend from sea to sea; that the great countries of Oregon and California are parts of the United States; and that from these countries, which are rich in gold and silver and precious stones, our steamers can reach the shores of your happy land in less than twenty days.
>
> Many of our ships will now pass every year, and some, perhaps, every week, between California and China; these ships must pass along the coasts of your empire; storms and winds may cause them to be wrecked on your shores, and we ask and expect from your friendship and your greatness, kindness for our men and protection for our property. We wish that our people may be permitted to trade with your people; but we shall not authorize them to break any law of your empire.
>
> Our object is friendly commercial intercourse, and nothing more. You may have productions which we should be glad to buy, and we have productions which might suit your people.
>
> Your empire contains a great abundance of coal; this is an article which our steamers, in going from California to China, must use. They would be glad that a harbor in your empire should be appointed to which coal might be brought, and where they might always be able to purchase it.
>
> In many respects commerce between your empire and our country would be useful to both. Let us consider well what

> new interests may arise from these recent events, which have brought our two countries so near together, and what purpose of friendly amity and intercourse this ought to inspire in the hearts of those who govern both countries.[5]

He then waited a week or so in the bay, during which time the squadron was provided with food and water and generally treated courteously. It should be noted that the entire time Biddle was at anchor, his two ships were surrounded by armed barges, boats, and hundreds of warriors. Biddle even allowed Japanese warriors to briefly board his ships, a decision for which he was later harshly criticized by U.S. authorities. On July 27, Biddle received from a response from the Tokugawa government. It reads:

> The object of this communication is to explain the reasons why we refuse to trade with foreigners who come to this country across the ocean for that purpose.
>
> This has been the habit of our nation from time immemorial. In all cases of a similar kind that have occurred, we have positively refused to trade. Foreigners have come to us from various quarters, but have always been received in the same way. In taking this course with regard to you, we only pursue our accustomed policy. We can make no distinction between different foreign nations—we treat them all alike; and you as Americans, must receive the same answer with the rest. It will be of no use to renew the attempt, as all applications of the kind, however numerous they may be, will be steadily rejected.
>
> We are aware that our customs are in this respect different from those of some other countries, but every nation has a right to manage its affairs in its own way.
>
> The trade carried on with the Dutch at Nagasaki, is not to be regarded as furnishing a precedent for trade with other foreign nations. The place is one of few inhabitants and very little business, and the whole affair is of no importance.

5. Robert Van Bergen, *The Story of Japan* (New York: The American Book Company, 1897), pp. 6, 192.

> In conclusion, we have to say that the Emperor positively refuses the permission you desire. He earnestly advises you to depart immediately, and to consult your own safety by not appearing again upon our coast.[6]

Japanese resolve in the matter was clear and Biddle had little choice but to accept the decision because his orders did not include the use of force unless it became necessary for self-defense. In an inexplicable turn of events, he then decided to hand deliver his own response to the Japanese flagship, unannounced, and was pushed or perhaps even struck by a Japanese guard. Suddenly, the event risked turning into an international incident. But cooler heads prevailed and violence did not erupt. Both sides recognized the precariousness of the situation. Biddle then issued orders to depart, having failed to establish relations but having achieved his goal of collecting information.[7] The Biddle visit made clear that however much the Japanese government might have tweaked or softened its policy on *sakoku* after the First Opium War, seclusion was still the law of the land. There would be no normalized commercial or diplomatic relations established unless the Japanese government changed its policy.

In 1849, U.S. policy changed from fact-finding to a more aggressive posture after the USS *Preble* visited Nagasaki in order to fetch sixteen U.S. castaways. The Japanese had treated the shipwrecked sailors poorly and some had died from exposure while in custody. Indeed, conditions were so intolerable that at least one of the sailors committed suicide. In this encounter, Commander James Glynn (1800–1871), captain of the *Preble*, simply would not be denied and used the full spectrum of negotiating tactics to win the sailors' release. He sailed boldly into Nagasaki Bay even when directed not to by the Japanese and positioned his ship so his cannon would do the most damage if it became necessary to use them. The Japanese refused to meet with him and demanded that he sail away. It also became clear that the Japanese were preparing a robust defense against this intrusion. Nonetheless, Glynn held his ground. He bluffed and cajoled his way to a meeting with Japanese officials, during which he secured the captives' release. Back home, the U.S. population was outraged when they learned of the sailors' ill treatment. President Millard

6. David Foster Long, *Sailor-Diplomat: A Biography of Commodore James Biddle, 1783–1848* (Boston: Northeastern University Press, 1983), pp. 213–214.

7. Long, *Sailor-Diplomat*, pp. 215.

Fillmore's (1800–1874) anger over the incident, combined with the realization that a resolute show of force had delivered results, drove a change in U.S. policy toward Japan (see Document 5).

In 1851, President Fillmore was determined that Japan would receive U.S. emissaries, even if the result was war. Fillmore instructed Commodore Matthew C. Perry to be well-mannered, but bold and persistent. If the Japanese refused to parley, he was to threaten the use of force and then, in the (likely) eventuality that force became necessary, open hostilities. This was gunboat diplomacy in its purest form—a completely different approach than that adopted by Polk when he sent Commander Glynn to Japan in 1846. Perry's orders read:

> If, having exhausted every argument and every means of persuasion, the commodore should fail to obtain from the government any relaxation of their system of exclusion, or even any assurance of humane treatment of our shipwrecked seamen, he will then change his tone, and inform them in the most unequivocal terms that they will be severely chastised.[8]

To prepare for the possibility of war, the U.S. squadron was augmented with large, capable ships—some of which employed the latest propulsion systems (steam engines) and most capable weapons. Perry was to ignore the diplomatic opportunities available at Nagasaki and head straight for the coastline nearest the seat of power—Edo Bay. Perry had learned much from Biddle and Glynn. Biddle had been open, accommodating, and quite visible. Glynn had been careful but uncompromising. Perry was to be aloof, hard-nosed, and even obstinate—not a stretch for Perry, who was already known to have some of these qualities.

Perry was also known to be an active promoter of U.S. expansion in the Pacific. In particular, he believed the Ryūkyū Islands had strategic value and could be easily seized. With both China and Japan laying claim to the islands—and with the Ryūkyū monarch attempting to accommodate both of those countries while exercising some authority of his own—it was not at all clear who had real authority over them, and this ambiguity could provide justification and legal cover for any Western country inclined to seize them. For Perry, the Ryūkyūs

---

8. Arthur Walworth, *Black Ships Off Japan: The Story of Commodore Perry's Expedition* (New York: A. A. Knopf, 1946), pp. 240–246.

would provide easy access to the Chinese mainland and could serve as an entrée into Japan. Once the United States controlled them, the Ryūkyūs could also be used as a supply station for whalers, a refuge for shipwrecked sailors, and a neutral port for exchanges. While en route to Japan, Perry wrote to John P. Kennedy (1795–1870), the U.S. secretary of the navy:

> As a preliminary step, and one of easy accomplishment, one or more ports of refuge and supply to our whaling and other ships must at once be secured; and should the Japanese government object to the granting of such ports upon the main land, and if they cannot be occupied without resort to force and bloodshed, then it will be desirable in the beginning, and indeed, necessary, that the squadron should establish places of rendezvous at one or two of the islands south of Japan. . . . The islands called the Lew Chew [*sic*] group are said to be dependencies of Japan, as conquered by that power centuries ago, but their actual sovereignty is disputed by the government of China. . . . [I]t strikes me, that the occupation of the principal ports of those islands for the accommodation of our ships of war, and for the safe resort of merchant vessels of whatever nation, would be a measure not only justified by the strictest rules of moral law, but which is also to be considered, by the laws of stern necessity, and the argument may be further strengthened by the certain consequences of the amelioration of the condition of the natives, although the vices attendant upon civilization may be entailed upon them.[9]

Perry's letter made its way to Edward Everett (1794–1865), the secretary of state, and eventually to President Fillmore. Fillmore made clear that the seizure of the Ryūkyūs should be a last resort and should only be attempted if the Japanese government responded negatively to Perry's broader mission. Part of Everett's letter reads:

---

9. Matthew Calbraith Perry, Francis L. Hawks, George Jones, and A. O. P. Nicholson, *Narrative of the Expedition of an American Squadron to the China Seas and Japan, Performed in the Years 1852, 1853 and 1854, Under the Command of Commodore M. C. Perry, United States Navy* (Washington, DC: A. O. P. Nicholson, 1856), pp. 105–106.

> The President concurs with you in the opinion that it is highly desirable, probably necessary for the safety of the expedition under your command, that you should secure one or more ports of refuge of easy access. If you find that there cannot be obtained in the Japanese islands without resort to force, it will be necessary that you should seek them elsewhere. The President agrees with you in thinking that you are most likely to succeed in this object in the Lew Chew [sic] islands. . . . It will attract a large share of the attention of the civilized world; and the President feels great confidence that the measures adopted by you will reflect credit on your own wisdom and discretion, and do honor to your country.[10]

Though Perry never seized control of the Ryūkyūs, his primary and secondary missions were clear.

After being selected to lead the squadron, Perry spent much of 1852 preparing for his visit. In addition to sailing on some of the U.S. Navy's finest steam-driven ships, he also wanted to bring with him a number of items demonstrating the industrial expertise and prowess of U.S. manufacturing. Perry was something of an expert on steam propulsion and had led several U.S. Navy attempts to adapt the technology to ships of war. Indeed, this expertise may have been one of the reasons he was selected to lead the mission. Finally, after waiting longer than he thought he should, he set sail for Japan in November 1852. After sailing through the Indian Ocean, the U.S. squadron arrived at Naha, in the Ryūkyū Islands, in May of 1853.

Perry's visit to the Ryūkyūs was relatively short but eventful. His men immediately set about surveying the waters off the coast of the main islands and he later sent a small force to reconnoiter the island of Okinawa. He undertook both activities without permission from the Japanese government. Perry demanded to meet the Ryūkyū monarch, Shō Tai (1843–1901), at Shuri Castle and appeared unbidden at his residence on two occasions. But Perry and Shō Tai never met. Perry's actions can be accurately described as heavy-handed, undiplomatic, and aggressive. The Okinawans appeared powerless to stop him and had to use their hard-won diplomatic skills—honed for centuries on

10. Perry, et al., *Narrative of the Expedition of an American Squadron to the China Seas and Japan*, pp. 108–109.

the Chinese and Japanese—in order to keep the peace. Indeed, the Americans acted more like a conquering force than a visiting expedition. Perry made no effort to camouflage his intentions; indeed, he hoped that word of his actions, posture, and demands—and that his next stop was going to be Edo Bay—would reach Edo. This hope was fulfilled. As quickly as possible, local authorities sent word to the Tokugawa that the U.S. squadron would soon be headed in that direction. The Japanese government was therefore aware, months in advance, of the U.S. visit and was not surprised when the squadron eventually arrived in Edo Bay.

Commodore Perry's Visit

On July 8, 1853, the American squadron of four naval vessels appeared off the coast of Uraga, near the mouth of Edo Bay. Two of the ships were steamers, and two were sailing ships. The Black Ships may have impressed some of the Japanese, but many government officials already knew what steam ships looked like—and the danger they posed. Perry had chosen his landing site well. Uraga was far enough away (approximately thirty miles) from Edo to reassure the Tokugawa that the squadron didn't pose an immediate threat to the seat of government, yet close enough that messages could still be sent quickly back and forth. However, given the ability of the U.S. vessels to quickly steam further into the bay (even against the wind), the threat to Edo was real.

The Japanese government fully recognized the precariousness of their situation. They were not in a position to forcefully oppose the squadron. If they opened fire—as they had on the *Morrison* fifteen years before—the United States might respond in kind, or even land a small detachment of Marines. But the domestic repercussions of engaging diplomatically with the United States could be significant. It was a situation fraught with peril for all sides if not handled carefully. In the end, the Japanese government was not sure how to respond most effectively. As they struggled to make decisions, they bought time by employing their old strategies of deflection, obfuscation, and delay.

When the U.S. squadron appeared off the coast of Uraga, Japanese officials sent several small vessels to inform the Americans they were to leave immediately (see Document 7). In similar situations in the past, the

Japanese used smaller boats to encircle, then put men aboard the foreign vessels. But Perry gave orders to repel any Japanese who attempted to board his ships and, after issuing a warning, threatened to fire on any small boat still in the vicinity. Perry indicated that he would not communicate directly with any Japanese representative who was not a "counsellor of the Empire."[11] Through lower-ranking officers, the Japanese made clear that Perry was to sail to Nagasaki. Perry, also working through lower-ranking officers, responded that he had purposely sailed to his current position and would not depart until he had delivered a letter from President Fillmore (see Document 10) directly to a high-ranking Japanese official capable of conveying it to the emperor (shogun). When Kayama Yazaemon, masquerading as the governor of Uraga (who was actually Ido Hiromichi [d. 1855]), pressed Perry to open a dialogue, Perry again refused.[12] As a compromise, Kayama suggested that he could accept Fillmore's letter but that Perry and the entire U.S. squadron would have to go to Nagasaki to receive a reply. Perry replied that he would not do this and that, after landing at Edo, he would hand-deliver the letter directly to the emperor (shogun). Soon thereafter, U.S. boats were seen surveying the bay. This aggressive move was meant to indicate that Perry intended to follow through on his threats (see Document 8).

Meanwhile, shogun Tokugawa Ieyoshi (1793–1853) was in no position to provide any direction in this encounter. Ieyoshi was not known for being a hands-on administrator in the first place. Several years before, he had turned the responsibility for day-to-day governance over to Abe Masahiro, one of his most able advisors. In addition, in July of 1853, Ieyoshi was on his deathbed (he passed on July 27). Abe was effectively Ieyoshi's temporary regent, but was, of course, restrained because he wasn't the actual shogun. Abe understood all too well how Japan's reputation as a forceful military government would suffer if it was unable to prevent a foreign foe from landing on its shores; he also knew that such an event would cause great consternation among the increasingly restive *daimyō*. But Abe could not risk the chance that the U.S. guns in Edo Bay might fire on the seat of government—or, even worse, that foreign troops might invade. Accordingly, Abe saw little

11. Perry, et al., *Narrative of the Expedition of an American Squadron to the China Seas and Japan*, p. 273.

12. This is an example of the extremely creative tactics the Japanese had used in negotiations with foreign emissaries in the past.

choice other than to accede to Perry's wishes and accept a letter from the U.S. president. On July 14, Perry landed with a small contingent of sailors and was met with great ceremony (see Documents 13 and 14). He delivered his letter and indicated that he would return in the spring. The Americans then sailed away.

The letter from President Fillmore to the emperor (shogun) was strikingly similar to the one sent with Commodore Biddle in 1846. The 1853 letter (see Document 9) simply expanded on the same themes: friendship; humane treatment of shipwrecked sailors; coaling stations; and, if possible, commerce. Much of the tone was similar as well, with one exception. President Fillmore, having heard of the ill treatment of the shipwrecked survivors picked up by the USS *Preble* in 1849, used unusually strong language for a diplomatic exchange. The phrase "we are very much in earnest in this" signifies the seriousness with which the U.S. government treated the situation. Though there was some room for maneuvering, the United States was indicating to the Japanese that there would be serious consequences if Japan did not treat its shipwrecked sailors well.[13]

Perry had succeeded in forcing the Japanese to interact with him outside the traditional diplomatic enclave at Nagasaki. But this was only the first step in the negotiations. Meanwhile, the Russians, who had been carefully monitoring events, sent a squadron of four warships to Nagasaki harbor. They arrived on August 21, roughly one month after the Americans arrived in Edo. The United States was aware of these Russian efforts and Perry, in particular, wanted to reach Japan first. The Russians were equally aware of American attempts. The threat posed to Japan in general by the four Russian ships was undeniable, but the threat to Edo was not the same as had been posed by the Americans. As had been the case in years before, the Japanese were initially able to delay and obfuscate Russian attempts at opening ports for trade and provisions—and, most importantly, the initiation of negotiations about borders in the islands north of Hokkaidō. But the expedition led by Admiral Yevfimiy Putyatin (1803–1883), like the Perry expedition, was ultimately successful. The opening of diplomatic relations between the West and Japan can therefore be understood best in the context of the Japanese government

13. Perry, et al., *Narrative of the Expedition of an American Squadron to the China Seas and Japan*, pp. 296–298.

responding to the demands of existential threats posed by multiple large empires.

The Japanese Response

Though not surprised by the arrival of the Americans and the Russians, the Japanese authorities still had difficulty processing the changing diplomatic landscape in the fall of 1853. It was clear that the United States was not going to be delayed for long and that Russia's attitude was hardening as well. There were few good options for maintaining the status quo. This was a dilemma many non-Western countries faced in the nineteenth century. If the targeted countries fought back against the imperialists, they would almost certainly lose not just the war but also their sovereignty. And if by some chance they won, their victory would likely only be temporary. Even with strong, effective leadership and a country united by common purpose, the struggle would have been extremely difficult. And Japan was anything but well led and unified.

The Council of Elders in Edo was divided on how to proceed. Accordingly, Abe Masahiro decided to poll the *daimyō* to gauge their mood and reach consensus on a plan. Such polls were rarely used. Abe provided the *daimyō* with a translation of Fillmore's letter and asked for their opinion on how to respond. There can be little doubt that he expected most *daimyō* would understand the gravity of the situation and accept his plan, which was to fortify coastal defenses and prepare for the worst while simultaneously engaging with the Westerners as grudgingly and carefully as possible. More than that, he hoped that the *daimyō* would agree to modify the policy of *sakoku* and provide him with the space he needed to keep Japan safe from foreign incursion. Instead, the *daimyō* appeared to be as divided as the Council of Elders. Some wanted to accommodate U.S. and Russian demands and open ports; others wanted to delay, then fight (see Documents 16, 17, and 18). Still others took the opportunity to harshly criticize Tokugawa leadership. Such criticisms would not have been tolerated just a few short years before. As the responses arrived, Abe realized his error in asking for support from the *daimyō*: his asking for help revealed just how weak the Tokugawa rulers were in the face of the foreign powers. In the end, there was no consensus. Abe had to make the final decision and bear the responsibility for its outcome.

When Perry returned to Naha in July, he forced Abe to accept an arrangement by which U.S. vessels could stop in Japan to resupply. He then wintered in southern China. While there, he learned that the French and British would be traveling to Japan as soon as possible to conclude agreements. With the Russians also attempting to normalize diplomatic relations with Japan in the summer and fall of 1853, the race was on to become the first European power in Japan. Accordingly, Perry met four other U.S. naval vessels (and two supply ships), some of which were among the most technologically advanced in the entire fleet. At this point, he commanded ten ships and at least 1,600 men. The combined U.S. fleet arrived on February 13, 1854. It was not lost on the Japanese that the Americans had arrived earlier than they said they would, and with even more ships and personnel.

Abe's gambit to poll the *daimyō* had been a waste of precious time, and the death of Tokugawa Ieyoshi had paralyzed the Council of Elders. Abe had not completed his preparations when Perry arrived and could thus only provide a partial response to the Americans. Abe was so worried he sent a message, through the Dutch, to Perry in southern China to ask for more time. Perry, however, understood this as yet one more effort to delay and obfuscate, and Abe's request was ignored. Indeed, Abe's request convinced Perry that the Japanese were not going to negotiate in good faith and that only a show of force would convince the Japanese to agree to U.S. demands.

Perry returned to Japan with a much stronger force. But he also perceived that the death of the shogun (and the subsequent difficulty in naming another) weakened the Japanese position in negotiations. Capitalizing on that weakness, he now expanded his list of demands to include items the Americans had initially wanted but for which they had not been willing to fight the year before. When Perry first arrived in 1853, the United States insisted only that Japan treat shipwrecked sailors humanely and find some way to transfer such sailors back to U.S. vessels. Abe agreed to this demand in 1854 and hoped that the United States would be appeased. But now Perry wanted to negotiate a broader treaty that would open ports to U.S. shipping, allow a diplomatic presence and limited commerce, and would provide some protection for U.S. citizens in Japan (see Document 11). After a few weeks of trying to delay, Abe correctly discerned that he had little choice and negotiated the best deal for Japan possible under the circumstances. Perry was asked to steam his squadron to Yokohama where the Treaty of Kanagawa was signed on March 31, 1854 (see Document 11). Perry and his squadron then returned home to great fanfare.

The Treaty of Kanagawa was the first of many "unequal" treaties forced on the Japanese. It opened two ports to the United States: Shimoda (on Izu Peninsula, south of Tokyo) and Hakodate (on the northern island of Hokkaidō) as coaling stations and ports for reprovisioning and trade. The treaty also established limited extraterritoriality laws for U.S. citizens in the ports and provided for U.S. consular representation. Perhaps most importantly, there was a most-favored-nation clause that allowed the United States to automatically enjoy any and all rights provided to any other nation in a future treaty. This treaty opened the door for many other Western nations: in August 1854, the British signed the Anglo-Japanese Friendship Treaty. The Russians signed in February 1855, the French in November 1855, and the Dutch in 1856. Japan's worst fears had been realized.

It was not initially clear to the Japanese that they had done more than open a few ports to foreign powers (see Document 20). The interior of the country was still generally off limits to foreigners, and Westerners did not pour into the port cities. Foreign soldiers did not take up residence, and walled compounds that were off limits to Japanese officials did not appear. It was only when, in 1856, the Americans sent a consul to Shimoda (as stipulated as a possibility in the Treaty of Kanagawa) that the Japanese government realized the extent to which conditions had changed (see Document 21). After many tense months of negotiations, in 1858 U.S. Consul Townsend Harris (1804–1878) negotiated the Treaty of Amity and Commerce with Hotta Masayoshi (1810–1864), Abe Masahiro's successor as head of the Council of Elders. Hotta recognized the difficulty he would have in selling this treaty to the *daimyō* and asked the (figurehead) Emperor Kōmei (1831–1867) to rubber-stamp it. The imperial household was trying to survive in a very fraught political environment, however, and demurred. Because of this failure to secure support, Hotta was ousted and replaced by his ally Ii Naosuke (1815–1860). Ii had followed the Second Opium War in China (1856–1860) and was cognizant of just how badly the war had gone for China; he did not want that to happen to Japan. He signed the agreement and effectively normalized diplomatic relations based on Western, imperial models. As before, other nations followed suit. In late 1858, treaties of amity and commerce were signed with the Dutch, Russia, Britain, and France (see Documents 22 and 23). These were more comprehensive, unfavorable to Japan, and unequal than the first set of treaties, increasing Japan's vulnerability and opening the country up to all manner of unseemly humiliations. Japan lost the ability to set its own policies, manage its borders, and control its own fate. Though not colonized in the strictest sense, Japan functioned as a semi-sovereign state at best. After the second round of treaties began to take effect, the domestic political situation began to deteriorate (see Document 24). Ii Naosuke remained in place as head of the Council of Elders. But the infighting and political intrigue that had been simmering just below the surface boiled over and plunged Japan into a period of political instability unlike any seen for more than 250 years. The second set of treaties did more to damage the Tokugawa government than had Commodore Perry's visits and the first set of treaties.

CHAPTER THREE
THE COLLAPSE OF THE TOKUGAWA SHOGUNATE

The five separate treaties Japan signed with the Western powers in 1858 changed the country in ways previous treaties had not. Though Westerners were at first slow to take advantage of their new extraterritoriality legal status, it was only a few years before they began to crowd into the eight newly established treaty ports and create their own foreign enclaves. The treaties stipulated that import tariffs would be collected by someone other than the Japanese government. This system, which was disadvantageous to Japanese commercial interests and deeply unpopular with the Japanese elites, was standard operating procedure for Western imperialist countries all over the world. Japanese anger and frustration—directed at the government that, in signing the treaties, allowed these intolerable changes to be foisted upon the country—began to grow. As a rule, the peasantry did not follow foreign affairs. Though they certainly noticed the appearance of foreigners, they tended to be curious, rather than antagonistic, toward the Western strangers. The anger directed at the Tokugawa government was coming from the ruling elites (at both the national and regional levels) and those wealthy merchants and financiers most affected by the economic and societal changes. Beginning as a general sense of confusion when the policy of *sakoku* was abandoned by the Tokugawa (see Document 19), over the course of the next decade the elites' sense of injustice built to frustration when the unequal treaties were signed; turned to anger at the growing feeling of national humiliation; led to opposition, then defiance and, finally, open rebellion. It is not possible to pinpoint the exact moment (day, month, year) when a critical mass of opposition had been reached. Nonetheless, the Tokugawa authorities were aware of the shift in sentiment and sought to forestall it.

Ii Naosuke (1815–1860), who became head of the Council of Elders after Hotta Masayoshi's resignation in 1858—and who shepherded the second set of treaties through to fruition—differed from his predecessors in many ways. He was a decisive and vindictive leader who, in the months just before and after the signings in 1858, initiated a campaign against any and all who publicly opposed him. He was careful to snuff out any meaningful dissent before it could flare up across the country. Among others, Ii targeted government officials and *daimyō* who promoted policies that were not in accord with his own. No one in the country was free to express their opinions regarding the government or its policies: not the purists (conservatives) who wished to maintain Japan's seclusion (*shishi* samurai), nor those who wholeheartedly embraced open borders.

The individual who perhaps best exemplified Japan's curiosity about the Western world during the period was Yoshida Shōin (1830–1859). Yoshida was a samurai from Chōshū domain in southern Honshū. Though little known at the time, he is now considered one of the most important intellectuals of the era. He was naïve, curious, audacious, rebellious, and surprisingly influential for someone whose life was so short. As a young man keen to learn about the West, Yoshida sought ways to travel abroad. When government officials denied his formal requests to leave the country, he attempted to stow away on one of the American ships anchored off Shimoda in 1854. Before attempting to board, Yoshida and his friend and protégé Kaneko Shigenosuke (1831–1855) handed some U.S. officers a letter to be delivered to Commodore Perry. It is translated below. The tone and content capture the curiosity many samurai felt regarding Westerners in this early period.

> Two scholars from Yedo, in Japan, present this letter for the inspection of "the high officers and those who manage affairs." Our attainments are few and trifling, as we ourselves are small and unimportant, so that we are abashed in coming before you; we are neither skilled in the use of arms, nor are we able to discourse upon the rules of strategy and military discipline; in trifling pursuits and idle pastimes our years and months have slipped away. We have, however, read in books, and learned a little by hearsay, what are the customs and education in Europe and America, and we have been for many years desirous of going over the "five great continents," but the laws of our country in all maritime points are very strict; for foreigners to come into the country, and for natives to go abroad, are both immutably forbidden. Our wish to visit other regions has consequently only "gone to and from in our own breasts in continual agitation," like one's breathing being

impeded or his walking cramped. Happily, the arrival of so many of your ships in these waters, and stay for so many days, which has given us opportunity to make a pleasing acquaintance and careful examination, so that we are fully assured of the kindness and liberality of your excellencies, and your regard for others, has also revived the thoughts of many years, and they are urgent for an exit.

This, then, is the time to carry the plan into execution, and we now secretly send this private request, that you will take us on board your ships as they go out to sea: we can thus visit around in the five great continents, even if we do in this, alight the prohibitions of our own country. Lest those have the management of affairs may feel some chagrin at this, in order to effect our desires, we are willing to serve in any way we can on board of the ships, and obey the orders given to us. For doubtless it is, that when a lame man sees others walking he wishes to walk too; but how shall the pedestrian gratify his desires when he seen another one riding? We have all our lives been going hither to you, unable to get more than thirty degrees east and west, or twenty-five degrees north and south; but now when you see how you sail on the tempests and cleave the huge billows, going lightning speed thousands and myriads of miles, skirting along the five great continents, can it not be likened to the lame finding a plan for walking, and the pedestrian seeing a mode by which he can ride? If you who manage affairs will give our request your consideration, we will retain the sense of favor; but the prohibitions of our country are still existent, and if this matter should become known we should uselessly see ourselves pursued and brought back for immediate execution without fail, and such a result would greatly grieve the deep humanity and kindness you all bear towards others. If you are willing to accede to this request, keep "wrapped in silence our error in making it" until you are about to leave, in order to avoid all risk of such a serious danger to life; for when, by-and-bye, we come back, our countrymen will never think it worthwhile to investigate bygone doings. Although our words have only loosely let our thoughts leak out, yet truly they are sincere; and if your excellencies are pleased to regard them kindly, do not doubt

> them nor oppose our wishes. We together pay our respects in handing this in. April 11.[1]

Not surprisingly, Yoshida and his companion were caught trying to board without permission. He implored the Americans to allow him to stay. Seeking to avoid a diplomatic kerfuffle, Perry declined to give them refuge. Arrested by the Japanese authorities, Yoshida and his compatriot were soon sent back to Chōshū. Kaneko Shigenosuke died in custody. Yoshida was placed under limited house arrest and spent most of his remaining years teaching at the family school. His stunt with Commodore Perry earned him some notoriety and helped him attract pupils.

Though Yoshida was known to be unpredictable, even mercurial, and prone to expressions of extreme emotion, he had the reputation of wanting what was best for his students and his country. His distinctive, idiosyncratic teaching style had him engaging directly with his students and challenging them to argue ethics and morality. The talks he delivered on Mengzi, the ancient Chinese philosopher, are perhaps his best-known works. Yoshida's teachings had an outsized effect on Japan—especially when one considers that he taught for only two years. Professor Umihara Tōru of Kyoto University wrote:

> Of the ninety-two men who studied at [Yoshida's] academy, two became prime ministers [Itō Hirobumi (1841–1909) and Yamagata Aritomo (1838–1922)], four were appointed cabinet ministers, and four reached the rank of prefectural governor or lieutenant governor. If one adds the twelve diplomats, justices, high ranking military officers, and technical experts who were given either imperial honor or court rank, the number of major success stories comes to twenty-two.[2]

Other of Yoshida's former students, including Meiji Restoration–era figures Kido Kōin (1833–1877), Takasugi Shinsaku (1839–1867), and

1. Perry, et al., *Narrative of the Expedition of an American Squadron to the China Seas and Japan*, pp. 485–486.

2. Umihara Tōru, *Yoshida Shōin and the Shōka Sonjuku: The True Spirit of Education*, vol. 2 (Bloomington: Indiana University Center for Research on Japanese Educational History and East Asian Studies Center, 2000), p. 2.

Kusaka Genzui (1840–1864) died prematurely—otherwise, they too would likely have risen to high government positions.

Yoshida was impatient, a man of action. He taught that pursuing knowledge without intending to make use of it was folly, and exhorted his students to improve society. Over time, his thinking on the Westerners—and their intentions for Japan—changed dramatically. When Yoshida opposed Hotta's attempt to gain Emperor Kōmei's (1831–1867) support for the Harris Treaty, he was charged with plotting to assassinate those he believed were betraying Japan through ineptitude or corruption. He was arrested, extradited to Edo, and executed there in 1859. While awaiting his fate, he entreated his students to actively oppose the government. He taught them it was their sacred duty to act on their beliefs—and when, a few years later, societal conditions worsened, his former students rose to help overthrow the Tokugawa. Yoshida became a symbol and martyr to many, and the *sonnō jōi* movement that called for a forceful response to any foreign incursion—even if that meant overthrowing the Tokugawa—grew out of his teachings (as well as the writings of a number of other loyalist samurai). The *sonnō jōi's* slogan—"Revere the Emperor, Expel the Barbarians!"—became a rallying cry for disgruntled samurai in the years after 1858.

It should be mentioned that Yoshida and others believed that the Emperor Kōmei in Kyoto might rally the opposition to the Tokugawa in the late 1850s. Japanese emperors had not wielded significant political power since the twelfth century. But the intervening centuries of military rule failed to dislodge the imperial line and Japanese emperors had come to enjoy a certain status as spiritual leaders and symbols of traditional Japan. Carefully navigating the political landscape of the late Tokugawa period, the imperial household was not keen to be drawn into any conflicts that could damage the institution. The Emperor Kōmei's handlers understood that being too closely aligned with seditious or rebellious opponents of the Tokugawa could bring ruin and hoped to emerge unscathed from the political machinations of the era. On the other hand, they recognized the weaknesses of the Tokugawa government.

Yoshida's 1858 arrest occurred during Ii Naosuke's counterrevolutionary action, now known as the "Ansei Purge." In this action—related, in part, to a dispute over the selection of the next shogun—Ii rounded up and arrested or imprisoned 100 men of high rank. Some of these men held positions within the shogunate; others were *daimyō*; some were even officials in the imperial household. Included were such influential men as Hotta Masayoshi and Tokugawa Nariaki (1800–1860; father of the final shogun). Political opponents were stripped of their positions and replaced by those loyal to Ii. Yoshida was executed along with seven other men. Elsewhere, Ii rolled back a number of initiatives put in place by Abe Masahiro and Hotta Masayoshi—initiatives that had granted the *daimyō* more freedom to administer and reform their own domains. Ii's efforts proved unpopular, both with the *daimyō* and with rich merchants, and alienated the very groups from which he most needed support. Ironically, he had given his opponents—increasingly radicalized samurai—more fuel for their fires.

At first it appeared that the Ansei Purge was a success for Ii and that it had stifled dissent against the Tokugawa. In the immediate aftermath, the number of public protests dwindled and public opposition to the treaties seemed less vocal. But ultimately the purge proved to have the opposite effect: Ii's actions succeeded only in driving the opposition underground, where they recruited followers and plotted their revenge. Loyalist samurai (*shishi*) and *sonnō jōi* leaders simply became more careful, cunning, and capable. Within months, Ii was cut down at the Sakurada gate outside the shogun's palace (now the Imperial Palace). His assassins were from Mito han and Satsuma han, two domains that were later to play significant roles in the Meiji Restoration. This is an instance when the death of a single man changed the course of history. After Ii's assassination, the Tokugawa never regained the political advantage and was incapable of finding leadership that could act decisively. From this point onward, the Tokugawa seemed to be outmaneuvered at all turns.

Following Ii's death, the Tokugawa softened its posture toward some of the more cooperative *daimyō*. It was the government's hope that working with the feudal lords would yield greater results than attempting to suppress them. The government even ended *sankin kōtai*, the system of "alternate attendance" that required all *daimyō* to live in Edo every other year—and in off years when they were back in their domains, leave their heir as a hostage in the city of Edo. Again, the effect of this decision was exactly the opposite of that which the government had been seeking: the end of *sankin kōtai* allowed the *daimyō* to return to their domains and plot insurrection. Meanwhile, the *shishi* samurai who had opposed Ii and the Tokugawa initiatives intensified their efforts to undermine and destabilize the government. They targeted foreigners whenever they had the opportunity, demonstrating the extent to which the government could not control them. Dozens of *shishi* attacks on foreigners occurred between

1860 and 1864, resulting in the deaths of several prominent Westerners, including Henry Heusken (1832–1861), translator for U.S. Consul Townsend Harris. In 1863, anti-Tokugawa radicals from Chōshū began firing on foreign ships passing through the strait separating the islands of Honshū and Kyushū. These radicals were led by Mōri Takachika (1819–1871), who had long been a thorn in the side of the Tokugawa (and who would continue to vex the government until it collapsed). Over the span of a few weeks in 1863, virtually all of the Western nations that had signed treaties with Japan had one of their ships attacked, and the passage was effectively closed. After several months of planning, the Westerners sent an international force of sixteen warships to chastise Chōshū. In September 1864, this combined force sailed into the strait, opened fire on rebel positions, and even landed a small detachment of troops. Though the fighting lasted two days, a single Japanese domain proved incapable of holding out against the combined Western fleet for very long. When the fighting was over, the Westerners demanded an indemnity (indicating the assumption of blame) the Tokugawa were unable to pay. When the Westerners then demanded—and received—additional treaty concessions in lieu of this indemnity, the central authorities in Edo were enraged. Though there had certainly been other incidents in which domain troops fired on foreign warships, this incident, and the Western response to it, was the most prominent of the era.

Samurai elements of Chōshū domain were actively working to destabilize the country through acts of terrorism, assassination, and open rebellion. One of the most significant of these acts began in July of 1864, when Chōshū samurai marched on Kyoto, ostensibly to free the Emperor Kōmei from Tokugawa influence. In 1863, the emperor had unexpectedly issued an order to expel the barbarians. To the Tokugawa, this was an unacceptable intervention in the affairs of state. But the emperor's order placed the Tokugawa in a difficult position because the government had no intention of carrying out the order. This left the Tokugawa open to accusations of treachery. The rebellious samurai were thus emboldened to act. Before the Chōshū rebellion was crushed, the Kinmon Incident of 1864, as it came to be called, caused the deaths of 450 people and the fires set by combatants destroyed tens of thousands of structures, laying waste to vast sections of the city. Outraged, the Tokugawa acted decisively against Chōshū. At least 130,000 samurai from southern Honshū and Kyushū converged on the domain to crush the opposition. Ironically, there was very little actual fighting and the domain capitulated quickly. Punishments were meted out and several ringleaders executed. The Tokugawa thought they had put an end to the rebellion and believed they had forestalled an existential threat to the government. But it soon became apparent that the Tokugawa had overplayed their hand and that the crackdown on Chōshū inspired parts of Satsuma (in addition to domains such as Chōshū, Mito, and Tosa) to join the struggle against the government.

While the southwestern domains strengthened their militaries and secretly plotted against the government, the Tokugawa were struggling to control an economy increasingly affected by the opening of the country. The surging export market benefited some. But it also drove up prices on many items. This was one of the factors contributing to Japan's rapidly escalating inflation; another was simply that the government, now essentially bankrupt, had debased the country's currency. These actions helped destabilize the economy and made a precarious situation even more unpredictable. When another famine struck Japan in 1866, tens of thousands rose in mass protests around the country to express their displeasure at the government response. There was even a major protest in the city of Edo. With the southwestern domains openly rebelling, the economy in freefall, and a general sense that the Tokugawa were incapable of governing effectively, it was increasingly clear—to a critical mass of samurai and commoners alike—that a change was necessary. All that was needed was a spark to light the flame of revolt.

In early 1867, the Emperor Kōmei, only thirty-five, died unexpectedly from what was very likely smallpox. After a period of mourning, the competition to name the next emperor began. For the previous two and a half centuries, the Tokugawa had not only named the emperor; they had also dictated the political positions that emperor would adopt. In return, the imperial household had nearly always supported the Tokugawa. Prior to this time, it would have been unthinkable that someone other than the Tokugawa might nominate an emperor. But these were not normal times for the shogunate.

The previous shogun, Tokugawa Iemochi (1846–1866) had effectively been a figurehead. When he died, the final shogun, Tokugawa Yoshinobu (1837–1913) assumed power. Yoshinobu had commanded the troops who put down the Kinmon Incident in Kyoto. A generally capable man, he implemented a number of reforms to the government and military. However, he did not have the support of significant numbers of important *daimyō* or of commoners all over the country. Yoshinobu agreed to name a fourteen-year-old boy, Mutsuhito (1852–1912)—later known by his reign name, Meiji—to the throne. Yoshinobu's plan to be the power behind Mutsuhito's throne did not succeed.

The rebellious domains continued to maneuver behind the scenes while these issues of succession played out at the shogunal and imperial levels. Realizing that Chōshū domain would continue to cause problems so long as its *daimyō*, Mōri Takachika (1819–1871), was in power, the Tokugawa again moved against him in 1866. This time, the Tokugawa shogun was forced to rely solely on his own troops because his allies in other domains decided not to participate in the action and only a few other samurai were willing to help. In a stunning turn of events, the Chōshū rebels ultimately repelled the Tokugawa troops. To *daimyō* around the country, the lesson to be learned from the event was this: if it could happen to Chōshū, it could happen to anyone. It appeared that the Tokugawa were attempting to regain the prerogatives and autonomy they had recently returned to the *daimyō*. It should be noted that just prior to this event, the new leaders of Chōshū domain and the leaders of Satsuma domain formed a secret alliance against the Tokugawa. (This explains, in large part, Satsuma's unwillingness to contribute men to the Tokugawa force sent against Chōshū.) The Tokugawa still believed Satsuma to be loyal. Some of the individuals who participated in the secret negotiations between Satsuma and Chōshū later became Meiji statesmen: Kido Kōin (1833–1877) of Chōshū, Ōkubo Toshimichi (1830–1878), and Saigō Takamori (1828–1877) of Satsuma. At the same time, Tokugawa troops were required to put down significant riots in Osaka and Edo, the two largest cities in Japan. The failed 1866 attempt to deal decisively with Chōshū's impertinence; the refusal of other *daimyō* to heed the call to arms; and, finally, social unrest on a large scale made clear that the Tokugawa were incapable of imposing order. The Tokugawa authorities were exposed as weak and feeble—a situation no government can long withstand.

Following the second Tokugawa action against Chōshū, representatives from Satsuma domain petitioned the Emperor Meiji for a letter pardoning the Chōshū leadership. This request put the imperial household in a difficult position. If they agreed to the punishment of the Chōshū leadership, they would be siding with the Tokugawa; yet pardoning the Chōshū leadership would put them in direct conflict with the shogun. In the remaining months of 1866 and most of 1867, the imperial household took very little action in either direction, although some former courtiers—such as Iwakura Tomomi (1825–1883), who served as chamberlain to Emperor Kōmei—openly called for the Tokugawa to be deposed. By this time the Tokugawa had alienated a critical mass of ruling elites and had demonstrated general powerlessness in the face of open opposition. The time was ripe for a formal challenge to their authority.

The events that led to the civil conflict known as the Boshin War were set in motion in the late fall of 1867 when small groups of samurai from Satsuma and Chōshū domains began to make their way to the Imperial Palace in Kyoto. On November 9, as part of a last-ditch effort to reorganize the government—and thereby prevent large-scale fighting—the *daimyō* of Tosa domain persuaded Tokugawa Yoshinobu, the last shogun, to resign his position and convene a governing council of *daimyō* from all over Japan (see Document 25). The leadership of Satsuma and Chōshū, however, refused to accept this compromise measure and forged a letter from the emperor to chastise Yoshinobu. Soon thereafter, samurai from Satsuma and Chōshū streamed into Kyoto. Yoshinobu, having correctly ascertained that his life was in danger, sent troops to Kyoto to wrest control of the emperor away from the rebels. But it was too late. Fighting occurred at the Battle of Toba-Fushimi in January of 1868, and Yoshinobu fled to Edo when the hopelessness of his situation became clear. He soon turned control of the shogun's palace over to a new military junta. The boy Emperor Meiji was restored to the throne by samurai from Satsuma and Chōshū domains, thus ending the era of Tokugawa rule. But it was unclear what the "Meiji Restoration" was to mean for Japan.

The Boshin War dragged on for another year and a half as Tokugawa loyalists were slowly defeated in one small battle after another. When the Battle of Hakodate ended in June 1869, the civil war was finally over. The Tokugawa shogunate had lasted more than two and a half centuries. It is accurate to say that the Tokugawa shogunate both collapsed internally and was defeated by external forces. The lack of large-scale fighting was indicative of a collapse. But it needed a forceful nudge to send it to the dustbin of history.

CHAPTER FOUR
THE DAWN OF THE MEIJI PERIOD

Overthrowing the Tokugawa was the primary goal of most participants in the Boshin War, and that goal was achieved quickly, even before the new leaders had the chance to establish a working blueprint for the new government. As the last pockets of Tokugawa loyalists were cleared out, the leaders of the new government met to plan their next steps. When, on April 6, 1868, the Emperor Meiji was placed on the throne (the formal Meiji Restoration), Kido Kōin (1833–1877) of Chōshū presented a document articulating the fundamental ideas to be adopted as guiding principles for the new state. This Charter Oath (see Document 26) set forth five precepts: (1) a desire to establish a representative assembly, (2) a call for unity and the inclusion of all classes in the affairs of state, (3) freedom for all classes to determine their own path in life, (4) the abandonment of evil (i.e., old) customs, and (5) a desire to use knowledge from abroad to strengthen the country.[1] These principles were as much a commentary on the weaknesses of the previous era as a road map for the new government. The Charter Oath made it clear that the new leaders would take the country in a different direction.

Under the new system, the Meiji emperor was to be the head of state. Given that he was only fourteen years old, however, it was extremely unlikely that he'd be taking on the responsibility of administering the realm on a daily basis, and Japan's new leaders never seriously considered giving him meaningful power in any case. The last time a Japanese emperor reigned *and* governed was in the fourteenth century—and his tenure had ended in civil war. Since that time, Japanese emperors did not govern; they really only *reigned* as figureheads. Real political power was held by the supreme military commander, most often a shogun. Without a shogun in power, the new ruling elites were forced to create a different political structure, one built upon the old imperial prestige-based system. The Meiji Emperor became something closer to a constitutional

1. John Breen, "The Imperial Oath of April 1868: Ritual, Politics, and Power in the Restoration," *Monumenta Nipponica* 51, no. 4 (Winter, 1996): 410.

monarch; not a puppet exactly, though he still had very little actual power. Real power was wielded, behind the scenes, by the Grand Council of State (*Dajōkan*) and codified in the provisional constitution of 1868.

The Grand Council of State is best understood as an oligarchy. The new government was composed of departments that functioned much like ministries. In this system, two dozen men—mostly from Chōshū, Satsuma, and Tosa domains—set policy and rotated through high-level positions as top administrators. They became known as the "Satchō clique." For a few years, the leaders of these departments had the title of "secretary," a title that was later changed to "minister." There was even a prime minister, though the government wasn't established as a British-style parliamentary system. These ministers (some of whom might or might not be in official positions at any given time) would reach consensus on a given issue and hand down decisions in the emperor's name. This opaque structure lasted, with some modifications, until 1890 when the Meiji Constitution finally took effect. For more than two decades, therefore, the Meiji oligarchs governed the country with minimal input from legislative bodies (although one met for a very short time) and largely free of public accountability. This gave them great autonomy and the power to reform the country. It also meant that full responsibility for development rested with a small group of men. They had to learn, quickly, what needed to change, what policies should be abandoned, and what new ones needed implementation. It should be noted that these oligarchs did not always agree with one another and power struggles sometimes occurred behind the scenes. In the early years of the Grand Council, at least two major disagreements spilled out into the public realm. One of these ended in the removal of Ōkuma Shigenobu (1838–1922) from government in 1881. The other resulted in a civil conflict (known as the Seinan War of 1877) and the death of Saigō Takamori (b. 1828)—one of the most beloved figures of the Meiji Restoration.

In the summer and fall of 1868, the new governing elites began to assess the condition of the country. They quickly came to realize that many of the ideas they had proposed and rallying cries they chanted in order to generate support were actually impractical and unattainable in the new Japan. The stark reality of Japan's economic and diplomatic situation was impossible to ignore and could not be overcome with simple sloganeering. Theoretically it was easy enough to "revere the emperor," but "expelling the barbarian" was an impossible task at that time. Lacking a military strong enough to defeat the combined Western forces, Japan would remain in its semi-sovereign condition. For the proud samurai who had defeated the Tokugawa, this was a bitter pill to swallow.

The new leaders of Japan were, as historian Peter Duus puts it, "not so very different from those they had overthrown."[2] Though conservative by nature, they were also realists. They had gained power, in part, by promising a return to past glory, but returning to the seventeenth century was impossible. Therefore, regressive policies were quickly abandoned. New, progressive policies were required to strengthen Japan and put it on the kind of sound governmental footing that would allow it to take charge of its own international affairs. Inspired by the slogan "*fukoku kyōhei*," the whole nation—commoners and elites alike—discussed and debated the best way to achieve the goal of "rich nation, strong army." The phrase—most closely associated with Ōkubo Toshimichi (1830–1878) of Satsuma, though he was only one of several oligarchs to embrace it—essentially means that national wealth makes a strong military possible. *Fukoku kyōhei* was not a new concept; references to similar ideas can be found in ancient Chinese texts as far back as the fourth century BCE.[3] From a politician's perspective, the slogan was a good choice because it was vague enough to allow for significant flexibility in the selection and implementation of policy—that is, any policy, no matter how radical, could be considered so long as it achieved the goal of "rich nation, strong army."[4]

The Meiji oligarchs decided to study the systems, institutions, and policies that made Europe and the United States strong, and to pick and choose those that might work best in Japan. Though innovative, this was a risky strategy. How much foreign ideology would the Japanese have to accept along with foreign systems? How many of Japan's "traditional" values would be lost? In exploring these questions, Japan's new leaders experienced a slow but fundamental shift in their philosophies; they went from being conservatives to radical revolutionaries. It should be noted that the Meiji revolution did not occur organically or bubble up from below. It was planned and carefully executed as the new leadership slowly came to understand that Japan's deep, systematic problems could only be

---

2. Peter Duus, *Modern Japan* (Boston: Houghton Mifflin, 1998), p. 85.

3. Richard J. Samuels, *"Rich Nation, Strong Army": National Security and the Technical Transformation of Japan* (Ithaca, NY: Cornell University Press, 1994), p. 35.

4. This is in contrast to Confucianism in which form and method are often understood to be as important as function and outcome.

solved through a total transformation of the country. But according to what blueprint would these institutions and structures be built? What would Japan look like when all the social and economic engineering was complete?

First, the Meiji oligarchs reorganized the Tokugawa feudal structure. In 1869, seeking a highly centralized, tightly controlled state—an idea for which they did not need to look abroad—they limited the absolute right of hereditary land ownership, and in 1871 they abolished domains altogether (see Document 27). They replaced privately held domains with larger, government-administered prefectures overseen by governors loyal to the new leadership. Initially, some of the old *daimyō* were made governors. But they were replaced within a few months with close allies of the governing clique.

The structure of the military had to be radically altered as well. In the Tokugawa period—when each domain controlled its own military force and each *daimyō* trained, supported, and commanded their own troops—the shogun called upon local lords to provide men when military action was required. But, as we've seen, these highly trained, well-organized, homegrown militias ultimately turned on the shogun and helped to topple the old government. Understandably, the new government wanted to ensure it would face no further organized domestic military resistance. Therefore, in 1873, Minister of War Yamagata Aritomo of Chōshū (1838–1922)—who, in the late nineteenth and early twentieth centuries, would become one of the most powerful men in Japan—established a new conscript army (see Document 28). Unless unfit for duty or able to buy an exemption, all Japanese males were required to serve in the military for a period of three years. Yamagata had traveled to Germany in 1869 and studied the Prussian system. He understood that military conscription did more than provide willing soldiers; it also helped instill in citizens a sense of loyalty to the broader nation, rather than to a particular region or domain.

This new, modern army was the future and the samurai now belonged to the past. Little by little—first with the post-Restoration abolition of the four classes, then the diminishment and eventual loss of all government stipends, and the creation of the national military—the samurai had no reason to exist. In 1876 they were stripped of all special privileges, including the right to carry swords. Finally, when the new conscript army defeated the rebels in the Seinan War of 1877, all hope of a samurai revival was ended.

The Iwakura Embassy (1871–1873)

Japan's new leadership could not forget or forgive the humiliation caused by the unequal treaties the country had been forced to sign between 1853 and 1868. But breaking free of the treaties would require that each one be revisited, examined, and reassessed before any action could be taken. Given the number of nations with which Japan's previous leadership had signed agreements, this process would take months, if not years, to complete. It would be a very long journey in both the literal and figurative senses. In addition to revisiting the terms of these treaties at the bureaucratic level, the Meiji leaders decided to undertake a general fact-finding mission. This ambitious embassy would visit such continental powers as the United States and Tsarist Russia and seek to renegotiate the terms of those unfair treaties. Oligarch Ōkuma Shigenobu first proposed the idea, likely at the suggestion of Guido Verbeck (1830–1898), a missionary with the Dutch Reformed Church (and eventual advisor to the Education Ministry).[5] This globe-trotting embassy was led by Iwakura Tomomi (1825–1883), an imperial courtier and influential leader in the Meiji Restoration.

Though the stated mission of the Iwakara Embassy was to renegotiate the unequal treaties, historians now see this journey as important for other reasons (see Document 29). More than half of the top leadership of Japan traveled to the United States, Great Britain, France, Germany, Belgium, Denmark, Sweden, Austria, Italy, Switzerland, and Russia (among other countries). Upon arrival in a new country, members of the embassy split up and traveled to different cities for the purpose of examining different aspects of that country's society, government, and institutions. The top leadership, however, spent most of their time visiting major cities in the United States, Great Britain, France, and Germany. Unsurprisingly, the Western authors of those unequal treaties were in no mood to revisit them, and no new agreements were successfully negotiated by Japan for another three decades. But the Japanese took the opportunity to examine Western models and later incorporated into their own government many of the ideas they learned about on the trip. Perhaps

5. Kume Kunitake, comp., and Martin Collcutt, trans., *The Iwakura Embassy: A True Account of the Ambassador Extraordinary and Plenipotentiary's Journey of Observation Through the United States and Europe*, vol. 1 (Princeton, NJ: Princeton University Press, 2002), p. XI.

most importantly, they came back with a clear sense of their own greatest weaknesses—and what needed to change before Japan could become a rich country with a strong army.

The members of the Iwakura Embassy were particularly interested in Germany and the ways in which Otto von Bismarck (1815–1898) and a small group of other Prussian leaders created a new political order. When they arrived, the Japanese ambassadors also discovered a Germany deep in the throes of the *Kulturkampf* religious and cultural struggle that eventually redefined the boundaries of German identity. This example of social engineering provided guidance on how to cultivate subjects loyal, first and foremost, to the state. The Japanese also carefully studied the Franco-Prussian War (1870–1871). Among the many lessons they learned from that conflict was that an aggressive military posture, carefully applied, can lead to success in foreign policy. Put succinctly, the German way of dealing with its neighbors was similar in outlook to the way the Japanese government wanted to deal with its neighbors. The Japanese found echoes of their traditional "warrior ethic" in Germany's approach to foreign policy and quickly adopted this stance as their own.

The Iwakura Embassy was warmly received by most of the nations it visited. The United States and Great Britain were especially friendly toward the Japanese ambassadors. The sheer size and strength of the United States—not to mention their past history with the Perry Expedition—fascinated the Japanese. The United States was a new nation, still determining its geographical boundaries, defining its cultural (and religious) identity, and industrializing rapidly. All of this was worthy of investigation by the Japanese delegation, who spent more time, by far, in the United States than any other country. The Japanese even sent several young women to be educated abroad. Some, such as Tsuda Umeko (1864–1929), completed university degrees in the United States and returned to Japan to become influential educators.

As the world's most heavily industrialized nation and the largest empire, Great Britain was also of intense interest. The Japanese were especially keen to study England's factories, transportation and communication networks, legal and political systems, religion—and, most importantly—navy. But the Japanese came away from both these countries unimpressed with democracy—that is, the control exercised by the population over the government. The Meiji oligarchs had seized control of Japan by force and were not keen to give the uninformed masses any meaningful control of the government. They were also unimpressed with the autocratic, anachronistic rule they found in tsarist Russia and were surprised by the extent of that country's relative weaknesses. For many Japanese delegates, the German model seemed to provide the most suitable example of "rich nation, strong army."

Within a generation, the Meiji leadership had adapted many different Western systems to fit the needs of Japan. Virtually no element of Japanese society was left unexamined or untouched. The new Bank of Japan was established on the Belgian model; France provided the basis for the police, judiciary, and newspapers;[6] Great Britain's postal system, telegraph system, and navy were copied; the army and (eventually) the Meiji Constitution were modeled on Germany's; and from the United States came blueprints for agricultural colleges, a national banking system, and (for a brief period) a primary education system.[7] This is just a short listing, and none of these models can be described as having been adopted wholesale or having remained static once implemented. They changed as conditions in Japan required.

Perhaps the most important lesson learned by the Iwakura Embassy was that Japan could catch up with the West if the Japanese people were willing to sacrifice to make it happen. Kume Kunetake[8] and the Japanese government ultimately compiled the embassy's findings in a 2,000-page document. This tome provided detailed information on conditions in the West and outlined the best, and fastest, means by which Japan could develop into a modern country. This summary of the embassy's findings was especially popular in the years immediately following its publication and is still studied as a model for developing nations. Of particular note, the account indicated that Japan was only perhaps forty years behind Great Britain in industrial development and thirty years behind the United States and continental Europe. This situation could be overcome with the careful application of Japan's considerable talent and energies.

---

6. D. E. Westney, "The Emulation of Western Organizations in Meiji Japan," in Peter Kornicki, ed., *Meiji Japan: The Emergence of the Meiji State* (London: Routledge Press, 1999), pp. 107–124.

7. D. Eleanor Westney, *Imitation and Innovation: The Transfer of Western Organizational Patterns to Meiji Japan* (Cambridge, MA: Harvard University Press, 1987), p. 13.

8. Professor and historian Kume Kunitake (1839–1931) was Iwakura Tomomi's private secretary on the Iwakura Embassy. By virtue of his position, he became the official chronicler of the journey.

Japan would then be ushered in to the ranks of the first-rate powers—or so its leaders hoped.

The Civilization and Enlightenment Movement

While the Meiji elites were traveling abroad, the average Japanese was just beginning to understand where—and how—Japan fit in the wider world. Many citizens developed a powerful curiosity about the West, the disparate collection of countries that had imposed their will on Japan a few years earlier. After two and a half centuries of relative seclusion, there was much for the Japanese to learn about the world. Initial anti-foreigner chauvinism was slowly overcome by sheer inquisitiveness. A new era seemed to be dawning, one in which virtually all segments of Japanese society were free to explore new ideas and new ways of thinking, most of which had been expressly forbidden for longer than anyone could remember. There was a flowering of culture and a willingness to experiment, to "try on for size" the ideas that shaped Western culture. For more than a decade, the desire to abandon the old and the traditional was palpable and ubiquitous. This was known as the Civilization and Enlightenment Movement (*bunmei kaika undo*).

Historically, the *bunmei kaika* movement has been understood as an idea espoused by the intellectual elites. While that's true, the movement also set the tone for Japanese society more broadly. In the middle of the nineteenth century, Japan had one of the most literate populations in the world: nearly 45 percent of men and 15 percent of women were fully capable of reading and comprehending the ideas being promulgated in the newly free press.[9] In the political chaos of the years just before and after the Meiji Restoration, new journals, pamphlets, magazines, and newspapers sprang up by the hundreds, spreading the ideas—some brilliant, some far-fetched, but all excitingly new—that had everyone

9. This is a topic about which there is little consensus among historians. One can argue through extrapolation from Ronald Dore's seminal work *Education in Tokugawa Japan* (Berkeley: University of California Press, 1965) for the figures above. However, in Richard Rubinger's *Popular Literacy in Early Modern Japan* (Honolulu: University of Hawaii Press, 2007), the author is careful not to provide percentages for the entire country, citing the limitations of fragmentary data.

talking. Debating clubs and learned societies also met regularly in the early and middle 1870s. The most prominent was the Meiji 6 Society (*Meirokusha*), established in 1873. The members of this group were well connected and counted among their number some of the most influential members of Japanese society. Many members, such as Nishi Amane (1829–1897), Nishimura Shigeki (1828–1902), and Katō Hiroyuki (1836–1916), were prominent educators; others, such as Mori Arinori (1847–1889), later became government ministers. The society discussed, among other things, religion, philosophy, politics, tariffs, transportation, democracy, the West, relations between husbands and wives, the nature of the Japanese language, the press, and education. Perhaps most importantly, they published a journal—the *Meiroku Zasshi*—that set the tone nationwide for discussion of these ideas. As with many other publications, the *Meiroku Zasshi* ended with the 1875 Press Ordinance law, which severely limited freedom of the press. The organization itself existed until the turn of the twentieth century.

The most widely known member of the Meiji 6 Society was Fukuzawa Yukichi (1835–1901). His work *Conditions in the West* (*Seiyō Jijō*), published in 1867, quickly sold 150,000 copies and was thereafter reprinted several times. It was the best-selling work of the age and made him a household name. It also launched his career as a public intellectual. He continued to write throughout most of his life and is known for his other early works, including the 1872 *Encouragement of Learning* (*Gakumon no susume*) and the 1875 work *An Outline of a Theory of Civilization* (*Bunmeiron no gairyaku*). The widespread popularity of these publications illustrates Japan's new openness to, and fascination with, all things Western. During this busy period in Fukuzawa's life, he also opened the academy that eventually became Keio University, today one of Japan's finest institutions of higher learning.

It is difficult to determine with certainty when the *bunmei kaika* movement ended. Some argue that when the new, highly restrictive press law began to be enforced in the late 1870s, the chilling effect on the press also did much to dampen general interest in all things foreign. Others argue that the backlash began in the late 1880s. Regardless, there was a reaction, and both the ruling elites and average Japanese returned to placing the highest value on Japanese identity and Japanese culture. The challenge for the Meiji elites, during the second wave of reforms in the 1890s, was to decide what exactly Japanese identity was, and what Japanese culture ought to be.

Conclusion

The connections between the visits by Commodore Perry and the collapse of the Tokugawa shogunate are undeniable. It was, however, somewhat incidental that the United States was the catalyst for the societal and governmental changes that swept across Japan in the years after the first visit. Tsarist Russia, Great Britain, or France, all of which were also trying to force their way into Japan, could just as easily have set that series of events into motion (and nearly did). But there was no coordination, and virtually no cooperation, between most of the imperialists; instead, there was friendly competition. Perry thus represented both a real and a symbolic challenge posed by the "West." This followed a trend seen in many other parts of the world because Japan, just like China, had not developed the organizational structures and industry necessary to defend itself. Because of this temporary imbalance, the Western nations could force their will on other peoples with little risk to their own positions and homelands. It is therefore impossible to overstate the role that the industrial revolution played on Western imperialism. The desire to dominate and control other peoples is evident in all human societies, but it is normally fettered by the horrible reality of war. Like the watershed moment 10,000 years ago when settled agriculture was developed, certain people groups simply adopted new technology and new ways of thinking sooner than others. It is important to note that early industrialization doesn't mean that Westerners were morally superior or somehow smarter than all others.

A nimble and well-led Tokugawa shogunate could have responded to the challenge posed by industrialization. But by the time the United States arrived, it was decades too late. Commodore Perry's challenge to Tokugawa authority stripped the veneer off of the government, exposing systemic weakness, corruption, and myopia. In the Tokugawa system, where "change" was forbidden by law, institutional limitations and poor leadership made it impossible to respond effectively. In the final analysis, internal dynamics, spurred on by external pressures, led to the Meiji Restoration.

Even with the Tokugawa gone, Japan was still in an extremely precarious situation. One wrong move in the first two decades of the Meiji period could have precipitated a crisis that resulted in the outright loss of sovereignty, followed by colonialization. (This is the sort of thing that nearly happened in India following the Sepoy Mutiny in 1857.) Japan's new leaders were wise enough to see that they had to adapt to survive and to recognize that piecemeal reforms would not suffice. They were also quick to abandon any real efforts to expel the Westerners or to reinstate the isolation they had enjoyed for two and a half centuries. By the end of the Meiji period in 1912, the new Japan was almost unrecognizable from the one that existed in 1868. The pace of change was dizzying, and the comprehensive nature of the reforms meant that little in society was left untouched.

Meanwhile, the Western powers did not remain static and industrialization continued for them in the second half of the nineteenth century. Great Britain's economy was still growing, but was slowly overtaken by the world's leading industrial colossus: the United States. Germany, France, and others continued to develop as well. Japan's effort to develop a "rich nation, strong army" had to keep pace with a target that was forever changing. The competition was neverending but the Japanese were more than capable of playing.

A NOTE ON HISTORIOGRAPHY

This book has two primary objectives: to introduce the history of Japan through the lens of the Perry visits and, in the documents section, to provide a more intimate perspective on the events that forever changed the trajectory of Japanese culture and civilization. The years covered in this book, approximately 1850–1877, saw Japan transformed from a secluded, anachronistic, semifeudal society into a more open, progressive, and increasingly prosperous country. It was the moment at which the cornerstone of contemporary Japan was laid.

One of the central arguments in this book is that the role played by the Western imperialists, though consequential, was not as all-pervasive as has been portrayed by many historians writing in English. This book therefore seeks to emphasize more of the Japanese perspective on Commodore Perry's visits. While it is true that the appearance of Commodore Perry changed the dynamic in Japan sufficiently to allow for the collapse of the old Tokugawa regime, it was the Japanese themselves who changed their government in 1868. Thereafter, it was the Japanese who met the challenge posed by the West by dramatically strengthening their economy and military and undergoing rapid industrialization. This work challenges the notion that the Japanese had little control over their own destiny.

The earliest works in English to chronicle the visits of Commodore Perry were penned by members of Perry's own embassy. The historical narrative that came to be established in the Western world was, therefore, U.S.-centered and largely portrayed the Japanese in a negative light. An example of these works is Matthew Perry's report on his expedition entitled *Narrative of the Expedition of an American Squadron to the China Seas and Japan, Performed in the Years 1852, 1853 and 1854, Under the Command of Commodore M. C. Perry, United States Navy* (1856). Thereafter, there were only a few English-language accounts of Perry's visits written by professional historians until Arthur Walworth published his popular work entitled *Black Ships Off Japan* in 1946. Walworth was a specialist in U.S. diplomatic history and, though his work was generally well received, did little to include the Japanese perspective. Histories perpetuating the U.S.-centered narrative continue to be published.

Examples include Peter Booth Wiley's *Yankees in the Land of the Gods: Commodore Perry and the Opening of Japan* (1990) and George Feifer's *Breaking Open Japan: Commodore Perry, Lord Abe, and American Imperialism in 1853* (2006). An exception is Mitani Hiroshi's *Escape from Impasse: The Decision to Open Japan* (2006), in which he gives a more Japan-centered account of the visits. Mitani's work, however, is a translation of a Japanese language work.

Japanese history specialists[1] have treated Commodore Perry's embassy more evenly and have tended to situate the visits in the broader Japanese historical perspective. However, there is a paucity of English-language works dedicated solely to Perry's visits that fall into this category, and most are used in Japanese history courses, which limits the audience and understanding of Japanese perspectives. Among the very few is Peter Duus' *The Japanese Discovery of America: A Brief History with Documents* (1997).[2] However, Duus' work is about much more than just Perry's visits. Other works penned by Japan specialists such as W. G. Beasley's *The Meiji Restoration* (1972) and Albert Craig's *Chōshū in the Meiji Restoration* (1967) provide a general narrative of Perry's visits, characterizing them as only one of many important events of the era. This is an approach also used by prominent Japan specialists who have authored textbooks on modern Japan such as Kenneth Pyle, Marius Jansen, and James McClain, among others.

Several well-known historians and world history textbook authors begin the story of modern Japan with accounts of Westerners making demands of Japan, but face serious challenges providing meaningful perspective on how the Japanese understood the events and how they responded based on the internal dynamic found in Japan itself. Even historians who have conscientiously sought to show the extent of agency the Japanese enjoyed and include non-Western narratives in their textbooks have sometimes struggled with these issues. For example, in *World History in Brief: Major Patterns of Change and Continuity* (2013), Peter Stearns mentions Commodore Perry and U.S. demands, but there is little indication that significant changes had already been taking place in Japan

1. These are scholars specializing in Japan who conduct research in the Japanese language and who publish in English.

2. Peter Duus' excellent book, *The Japanese Discovery of America*, is now out of print.

before Perry's arrival.[3] Except for the new figurehead Emperor Meiji, Stearns mentions no other Japanese person in his long unit on Japan from the 1850s to the First World War. Conversely, Stearns' section on Russia during the same time period chronicles many historical actors and events initiated by the Russians. William Duiker, in his *Contemporary World History* (2014) textbook, provides some broad historical context of the domestic situation in Japan, but mentions only one Japanese person: Prime Minister Itō Hirobumi, who was responsible for initiating *any* of the momentous historical events over the second half of the nineteenth century. Yet in the same chapter, Duiker names seven different Westerners who influenced Japan.[4] For such historians, the Japanese remain largely anonymous and without agency outside of the Western historical narrative. By way of contrast, this new book uses the well-known account of Commodore Perry's visit as a starting point for students of Japanese history, taking them on a journey from the familiar to the unfamiliar. But it places the Japanese perspective at the center of the narrative.

3. Peter Stearns, *World History in Brief: Major Patterns of Change and Continuity*, 8th ed. (Upper Saddle River, NJ: Pearson, 2013), pp. 485–503.

4. William Duiker, *Contemporary World History*, 6th ed. (Boston: Wadsworth Press, 2014), pp. 58–65.

DOCUMENTS

Document 1

The Diminishing Resolve of the Samurai in Late Edo Japan (1796)[1]

Samurai ranked at the top level of the social structure in the Tokugawa period (1600–1868). Their occupation was to train for war and to keep the peace. They were only allowed to work other jobs as specified by the shogunate and, in particular, were not to labor in professions reserved for peasants, laborers, or skilled craftsmen. Merchants were at the very bottom of the social structure and it was considered shameful for samurai to work jobs reserved for such lowly merchants. When samurai were forced to work such jobs in order to survive, it led to personal dishonor and exposed the incongruity between the Tokugawa ideal society and the necessities of real life. The increasing number of warriors who were unable to maintain the samurai ideal as the Tokugawa period progressed indicated that the system wasn't working as designed.

It is difficult to maintain a sincere heart for those called "samurai." Their normal income is insufficient and, unintentionally, they bend the knee to even peasants and merchants. They slowly become anxious and humbled, endure their daily hardships and get by selling their handiwork. It seems as though their samurai spirit declines, like someone made to push a cart uphill. It diminishes day after day, month after month.

---

1. "Decline in Samurai Morale, 1796." Takano Tsunemichi, *Shōheiyawa* [Evening Talks on the Peaceful Condition of Our Times], in *Ishinshi* [A History of the Meiji Restoration], vol. 1 (Tokyo: Meiji Shoin, 1939), p. 329. Translated by the author. Originally found in David J. Lu, *Japan: A Documentary History* (New York: M. E. Sharpe, 1997), p. 277.

Document 2

Infanticide, Abortion, and the Effects of Poor Leadership in Agriculture (1827)[2]

Agricultural societies have always been plagued by periodic famines caused by droughts, floods, war, and general pestilence. But the unknown author of this document claims that systematic neglect of the agrarian sector in Tokugawa Japan was the cause of a famine. The author asserts that the lack of government leadership in the agricultural sphere caused unspeakable hardship, including the selling of tens of thousands of children into prostitution, numerous abortions, and frequent infanticide. This was an abomination for which the country would pay a divine price. He calls on the Tokugawa leadership to provide leadership to the peasantry and to follow the moral guidance of the Confucian ethic. He blames the leaders of the country for a "lack of compassion," a moral failing in Confucian philosophy. Such bold and open criticism was extremely dangerous under an authoritarian regime. It could have led to judicial sanction including fines, property confiscation, imprisonment, or even execution.

Since the Middle Ages agricultural guidance in the various provinces has been on the decline, there having been no appointment of farm experts to study and to assist the people in the development of natural resources. Thus, despite the beauty of our country and the abundance of fertile land, the exhaustion of the soil and the lack of new attempts at cultivation have led to a scarcity of products, which are hardly sufficient to feed and clothe the populace of the country. This, in turn, has led to difficulty in rearing children and to the secret practice of infanticide. The practice is particularly widespread in the northeast and in the eastern regions. It is also widespread in the Inland Sea region, Shikoku and Kyushu, but there the children are killed before their birth, thus making it appear that there is no infanticide. The one place where infanticide seems to be extremely rare is Echigo, but in its stead the practice prevails on a large

2. Satō Nobuhiro, "The Population Problem," *Keizai Yōroku, 1827* [The Essence of Economics, vol. XVIII, pp. 433–434]. Translated by Wm. Theodore de Bary, *Sources of Japanese Tradition*, vol. II (New York, Columbia University Press, 1958), pp. 65–66.

scale of selling girls over seven or eight years of age to other provinces for prostitution. In fact, girls for prostitution is a kind of "special product" of Northern Echigo. Some consider this practice inhuman, but to think so is a great mistake. It is far more humane than either abortion or infanticide. I was told that long ago in Central Asia there was a large country whose king killed 3,300 children annually to obtain their livers, with which he made a medicine for the kidney to be used for sexual purposes. No one who is told of this practice can help but feel a sense of shock and revulsion. When first I heard of it, I too was greatly shocked, but later, as I reflected on it deeply, it occurred to me that while the king's act of slaying 3,300 children annually was indeed inhumane, it was not as barbarous as the practice of infanticide which is prevalent today. In Mutsu and Dewa alone, the number of children killed annually exceeds sixty or seventy thousand. And I have not yet heard of anyone who deplores this situation. I find it nonetheless an unspeakable state of things. . . . That infanticide is so widespread in the various provinces cannot be attributed to the inhumanity of the parents. In the final analysis, it must be attributed to the ruler who lacks compassion, who is unaware of his duty as deputy of Heaven to help the people, who does not study the science of developing natural resources, who does not appoint agricultural experts, and who fails to carry out a program of agriculture which would encourage farmers to exert their utmost. Under such rule agricultural yields are meager and the condition of the land poor. Human beings are the beloved children of heaven. If rulers fail to carry out the teaching of service to Heaven, and permit the slaying of several tens of thousands of children year after year, who knows what Heaven will not do? If this state of affairs continues, divine punishment is inevitable. Therefore the ruler of the land must not fail to adopt methods for the achievement of national prosperity.

Document 3

Ōshio Heihachirō's Public Proclamation as the 1837 Uprisings in Osaka Began[3]

During the 1830s, Japan endured a period of extreme hardship known as the Great Tempō famine. Hundreds of thousands of Japanese citizens died from starvation and malnutrition. The government was unwilling and unable to respond in an effective manner. As a samurai, police constable, Confucian scholar, and former government official, Ōshio had a unique perspective on the corruption, incompetence, and callousness of the Tokugawa regime. He was indignant with the tepid response of the authorities and pleaded with them to provide assistance. Yet they would not. Moved by the suffering of his countrymen, he sold most of his possessions to help the destitute. He then led an uprising in the Osaka area that, while ultimately crushed by the government, captured the imagination of many in Japan. The Tempō famine is understood to be a turning point in the late Tokugawa period. From that time onward, the population of Japan was much less willing to support the shogunate than they had been previously.

If the four seas suffer destitution, the beneficence of heaven cannot long survive. If a man of small stature governs the country, calamities become inevitable. These are the teachings bequeathed by the sage of old to the later generations of rulers and subjects. The Deity enshrined in Tōshōgu (the spirit of Tokugawa Ieyasu) decreed that to show compassion for the widows, widowers, and the lonely is the foundation of benevolent government. However, during the past 240 to 250 years of peace, those who were above gradually became accustomed to luxury and they now live in sheer extravagance. Those officials who are entrusted with important political affairs openly give and receive bribes. Some of them who lack virtue and righteousness still attain high positions as a result of connections they have through the ladies in waiting in the inner palace. They level an excessive amount of money from common people and farmers in

3. Fujimoto Kunihiko, "Ōshio Heihachirō's Manifesto, 1837," *Nihonshi: Shiryō Enshū* [A Japanese History: Documentary Exercises]) (Tokyo: Tokyo University Press, 1956), pp. 289–291. Found in Lu, *Japan: A Documentary History*, pp. 280–281.

their own domains or administrative districts. These are the people who have suffered over the years the severe exactions of annual taxes and various types of corveé labor. Now they propose such nonsensical demands. As the needs of those officials increase, the poverty of the four seas is compounded....

The excessive rise in the price of rice today does not deter the commissioner in Osaka and his officials from engaging in their arbitrary handling of policies, forgetting that everything under the sun is one in the way of human heartedness. They transport rice to Edo, but fail to make any provision for delivery of rice to Kyoto where the Emperor resides. Instead they even arrest those people from Kyoto who come to buy rice in the amount of five to ten quarts....

The rich in Osaka have over the years made profitable loans to the *daimyō* and seized a large sum of gold, silver, and stipend rice in interest. They now enjoy unprecedented riches, and even though they are merchants they are treated and appointed to positions comparable to the elders in the households of the *daimyō*. They own numerous fields and gardens and newly cultivated fields and live in plenteous comfort. They observe the natural calamities and punishments of heaven occurring now, but are not afraid. They see the poor and beggars starve to death, but do not lift their fingers to help them. . . . Meanwhile they continue to indulge in their pastime, and act as if nothing has ever happened. This is not different from King Zhou's long night feast.[4] The commissioner and his officials have the power to control the actions of the above mentioned people and help the lowly. But they do not do this, and day after day deal in commodities. They are bandits stealing the beneficence of heaven, whose actions cannot be condoned by the Way of Heaven or by the will of the sage (Confucius).

We who are confined to our homes find it is no longer possible to tolerate these conditions. We lack the power of King Tang and King Wu.[5] We do not have the virtue of Confucius or Mencius. For the sake of all under heaven, knowing that we have no one to depend on and that we

4. This was an insult to any ruler in East Asia. King Zhou was the last king of the Shang Dynasty in China (1600 BCE–1046 BCE). King Zhou was remembered by Chinese Confucian elites as the embodiment of what a ruler should *not* be. He was described as hedonistic, capricious, decadent, cruel beyond measure, and totally uninterested in governing the country.

5. Examples of good kings in classical Chinese history.

may impute the punishment to our families, those of us who are of like mind are resolved to do the following: First we shall execute those who torment and harass those who are lowly. Next we shall execute those rich merchants in the city of Osaka who are accustomed to the life of luxury. Then we shall uncover gold and silver coins and other valuables they hoard as well as bags of rice kept hidden in their storage houses. They will be distributed to those who do not own fields or gardens in the domains of Settsu, Kawachi, Izumi, and Harima, and to those who may own lands, but have a hard time supporting fathers, mothers, wives, and other members of the family. The above money and rice will be distributed. Thereafter as soon as you hear that there is a disturbance in the city of Osaka, mind not the distance you travel, come immediately to Osaka.

What we do is to follow the command of heaven to render the punishment of heaven.

Eight year of Tempō (1837) month, day

To the village officials, elders, farmers, peasants, and tenant farmers in the domains of Settsu, Kawachi, Izumi, and Harima.

Document 4

Excerpt from "Report of Captain Lindenberg, of the Russian American Company's Ship *Prince Menchikoff*, to the Commander of the Colony of Sitka, October 17, 1852"[6]

The Japanese government policy of sakoku *prohibited unauthorized foreigners from visiting Japan. But it also prevented Japanese who had been shipwrecked outside of Japanese territorial waters from returning to their home country. This document relates the story of a Russian commercial vessel's attempts to repatriate unfortunate Japanese castaways, and illustrates the human toll of Japan's foreign policy. It should be noted that the Russian captain refused to go to Nagasaki where he might have succeeded in returning the unfortunate sailors. The Russian response to the Japanese vice-governor of Odawara, however, makes clear that the Russians had ulterior motives and wanted to use this opportunity to test the policy of* sakoku. *The Japanese appear to have been aware of this ruse. The fate of the returned Japanese sailors is unknown.*

On the evening of the 1st of August, while there was still some daylight left, several divisions on horse and foot passed along the road by the seashore, and as it grew dark, we could still perceive that numerous columns were marching along the road opposite the ship, moving from the country toward the town. When we asked Japanese what was the meaning of all this, they replied that the Governor of Odawara—a very important officer—was about to arrive, and that he never moved anywhere without being accompanied by at least 700 troops.

On the following morning the Vice-Governor of the city of Odawara came to the ship, accompanied by a large number of barges. When he had mounted the deck he summoned our Japanese to him, and when

6. "Report of Captain Lindenberg, of the Russian American Company's Ship *Prince Menchikoff*, to the Commander of the Colony of Sitka, October 17, 1852." Found in and translated from the *New York (Weekly) Tribune*, December 24, 1853.

they knelt round him in a half circle he made them a long speech, while all those whom he had brought with him remained standing, but bowed their heads low, out of respect to what he was saying. When he had finished his address, sadness and sorrow were evidently visible on the countenances of our Japanese, and they were also apparently very much perplexed, some of them indeed wept aloud. When I asked what this meant, one of them informed me that the Governor had explained to them that he could not receive them, and that they must return with us. This conclusion was very difficult for our poor Japanese to bear, as it was so entirely unexpected, for ever since our arrival it had always seemed that our object would be readily obtained. As I did not choose to enter into any explanation with the Vice-Governor upon the deck, I invited him down into the cabin, where he assured me, that according to orders received from Yedo [Edo/Tokyo], he could neither receive the returned Japanese nor the letter which I had brought with me; that as the port we were then in was not intended to be entered by foreigners, he could no longer hold any intercourse with me; and, finally, in accordance with the strict orders he had received from his Government, he begged to inform me that as there was now no reason why I should remain any longer in the harbor, that he had to request I would at once take my departure. Fruitlessly I placed before him the unreasonableness and even cruelty of his conduct toward his countrymen, and his ingratitude toward the Russians, who had undertaken a long and tedious voyage for the one good object of returning some unfortunate, shipwrecked sailors, who had, much against their own will, passed two years and a half away from their own land, back to their homes; and at length I told him, even if we did not take the Japanese back again to Russia, that the following year another vessel would be sent, and that they would then be obliged to receive them, to which he answered that next year and forever the answer would be the same; that it was the order of the Government, and that he himself could do nothing. It was easy to see, however, as well on his countenance as on those of his companions that his own opinions did not coincide with the orders he was obliged to obey. I now declared my wish to have a personal interview with the Governor of Odawara, in order to receive my answer from him; but the Vice-Governor persisted that this was utterly impossible, and that he had been sent on board the ship in order to make me acquainted with the final decision of the Government, and finally he pressed me to leave the port as soon as I could, especially as the wind was favorable. He pointed out at the same time how very much our ship had been favored, inasmuch as a very important section of the Japanese law had been broken, namely the one that forbade any armed vessel making any stay in the ports of the Empire; and that hitherto all armed vessels that had visited their port had been compelled to give up all their ammunition, weapons, and even their rudders. He told me that I could take the Japanese sailors to the Port of Nagasaki, and try if they would receive them there; but as this would have seemed like retreating, I assured them that I had no orders to go to Nagasaki from my Government, and as I had been commanded to put the Japanese on shore at Shimoda, I should have them put into a boat and carried to the land. Believing that I intended to do this while still in port, he sprang up from his chair and uttering a cry, declared that it was impossible, and expressed a wish to go at once on shore. I held him back, however, and said that as I did not wish to disturb, in any way, the friendly relations existing between the Japanese and Russian Governments, I would not break the law, but as it was absolutely necessary that I should complete the orders given me by my own Government, and land the Japanese, I would do so at some other place, as they objected to my doing it there. To this he answered, that he did not know whether this was possible or not, but that he was not answerable for any stoppage I might make after I had left the harbor. Outside the port, indeed, I could do what I choose, but now he begged me at once to set sail and quit the harbor as soon as I could.

As I deemed it imprudent if not impossible to land the Japanese by force, and also saw no means of conveying the letter into the Governor's hands, I determined not to have any quarrel with them; although I do not suppose the anger of the Japanese would have been so very formidable, yet I did not choose, as I had no means of meeting force with force, to expose the Russian flag, and consequently I saw no other mode of proceeding open to me than to retire. Therefore I told the Vice-Governor that as he did not choose to receive his countrymen and would not hold any further intercourse with me, I had nothing more to do, but should proceed to sea at once and put the Japanese on shore somewhere in the neighborhood. He then ordered twenty of the largest boats near the ship to assist in getting us round, and taking his leave in a friendly manner, proceeded on shore with all his followers. When we had got round the little island we set our sails, and having dismissed the boats, steered out of the bay.

As we proceeded out of the harbor the Japanese told me that they did not wish to go any further with us and begged to be put at once on shore even though they might immediately be killed. As I saw that it was useless to take them to China with me where it would have been impossible to have concealed them from want of room in the ship, which was only intended for the conveyance of tea, I determined to do as they wished, and steering quietly along the shore, chose a small bay about twenty miles from the port in order to land the Japanese in two boats which we had brought with us for this purpose. When they were about to leave us they thanked us on their knees and with tears for the kindness which the Russians had shown them, and then jumping with every appearance of great joy into the boat, went toward the shore. When they had landed at a small village which was at the bottom of the Bay, we set our ship again on her course and steered according to our instructions, direct for China.

Document 5

Report from St. Helena—Cruelty of the Japanese toward American Sailors[7]

By the nineteenth century, Japan's policy of treating all foreigners who arrived in Japan without permission as criminals had become intolerable to many Western countries. Even shipwrecked sailors were incarcerated and faced uncertain futures. The account below reached the desk of President Millard Fillmore, who became indignant at the unnecessary death of a U.S. citizen. He held the Japanese government directly responsible. President Fillmore determined to persuade the Japanese government to treat shipwrecked sailors humanely until they could be returned. The case below provided the final impetus for Fillmore's fateful decision to send Commodore Perry to Japan. Perry's orders were, above all else, to obtain an agreement safeguarding castaways. If the Japanese government refused, Perry was authorized to demonstrate U.S. resolve by the use of force.

By the bark *Eureka,* arrived from Canton, this morning, we have the following statement of the cruel treatment by the Japanese toward shipwrecked American seamen, and the murder of one of the unfortunate men taken from St. Helena some months ago:

Murphy Well, an American citizen, born in the State of New York, late carpenter on board the American whaling ship *Lawrence,* of Poughkeepsie, Capt. Baker, states that the vessel (*Lawrence*) was wrecked on the 18th of May, 1846, by running on the reef of rocks, in the dead of night, about 300 miles off the coast of Japan, during very thick weather. All hands remained by the vessel till daylight, when three boats were manned, by the whole of the ship's company, who took with them all of their clothing, &C., that could possibly be got at, as the vessel was fast going to pieces, the sea making the breach over her. They made the best of their way for the Island of Japan. During the night the boats separated, and the two of them have never been seen since.

7. *New York Daily Times,* June 15, 1852, p. 2. Originally found in Peter Duus, *The Japanese Discovery of America,* pp. 71–72.

Our boat (*Wells'*) arrived in safety, after seven days' passage. On the moment of arrival, the natives took possession of all of us, our boat and effects, and we were thrust into a prison cage, made similar to those in which wild beasts are kept for exhibition, where we were confined and half starved for *eleven months and a half*, after which we were transported to a Dutch settlement down the coast, where we were again put in prison by the Japanese for two months more.

At the expiration of this confinement, we were brought before the chiefs and tried for daring to approach their land. We told them we were shipwrecked, which they would not listen to, and upon no terms would they grant us our liberation. They threatened to cut off our heads, because they thought we were English, whom they hate; but when we *told them we were Americans*, they said nothing more, except to ask us of what religion we were. Upon our telling them we worshipped GOD, and believed in JESUS CHRIST, they brought a cross bearing the image of our Saviour, and had we not trampled upon it at their request, they would have massacred us on the spot. We were then detained on shore, in prison, for a couple of days more, when they sent us on board a Dutch ship, bound to Batavia, where we arrived in December, 1847—each of us doing the best we could for ourselves to get a passage home.

While we were in Japan, in prison, one of our comrades, THOS. WILLIAMS, endeavored to make his escape, but was caught and taken back to prison in a dying state, owing to wounds inflicted on him with some deadly weapon; there was a gash over his forehead which bled profusely. The poor fellow lived about six hours. The natives brought a coffin, into which they compelled us to place the corpse, when they took it away. What was done with it, we could never ascertain.

The names of those saved from the wreck are GEO HOWE, second mate; THOS. WILLIAM, seaman (since murdered); THOMAS WILLIAMS, seaman; PETER WILLIAMS, seaman; HENRY SPENCER, seaman; MURPHY WELLS, carpenter.

We heard of several English seamen being there in confinement similar to ourselves.

It is *anxiously hoped the American Government will* not suffer this treatment, but more particularly, so sanguinary an act towards hapless shipwrecked American seamen to pass without ample retribution.

Document 6

The Path to Profligate Living of Samurai New to Edo, 1855[8]

The warrior ethic (bushidō) *reflected a rural sensibility. A frugal lifestyle combined with obedience to one's lord, regular military training, and honorable conduct were hallmarks of the ideal. The passage below illustrates how rural samurai were led to hedonistic habits in the late Tokugawa period.*

The permissive (samurai) who have come to Edo to work are mostly introduced to it by samurai (already) on duty. The living standards of samurai on regular government duty diminish and remember that, from childhood, they got by doing occasional jobs at home. They are raised with no education and spend money they find in their pockets. Many regard this as the Edo sensibility. The newly arrived rustics who come to Edo are scorned, an unyielding spirit develops and they wish to become a man about town. They are guided and dragged into the circles of debauchery.

8. "Corruption of Samurai, 1855." Translated by the author. Fujimori Taiga, *Shinseidan* [A New Treatise on Politics], in *Ishinshi* [A History of the Meiji Restoration], vol. 1 (Tokyo: Meiji Shoin, 1939), p. 323. Originally found in Lu, *Japan: A Documentary History*, p. 276.

Document 7

First Contact (1853)[9]

The American sailors who arrived at the mouth of Edo Bay in 1853 as part of the U.S. East India Squadron did not know how they would be received by the Japanese. Accordingly, they made every preparation for battle should they be rebuffed. Commodore Perry's orders were to do everything in his power to keep the peace—but also to wrangle an audience with a high-ranking Japanese official. If necessary, he was to use force as a demonstration of U.S. resolve. The passage below illustrates just how fraught with peril this first encounter was. One careless or foolhardy move by representatives of either side would have led to bloodshed.

At sunset on Thursday, the 7th of July, the squadron was, according to observation, about forty miles from Cape Negatsuo, or Idzu, as it is otherwise called. The heads of the ships were put off shore from midnight until four o'clock next morning, when the first sight of Japan was obtained from the mast-head. Although the morning was fine, the atmosphere was so hazy that there was but an indistinct view of the outline of the precipitous coast. Through the mist, however, the bold promontory of Idzu could be seen rising loftily from the sea, and stretching back in a crowd of mountainous elevations, while to the eastward lay Tosi-Sima, Likene-Sima, and other islands of the Broken Group, which are scattered along the coast of Japan.

The course of the squadron was now pointed directly to the entrance of the bay of Yedo [Edo/Tokyo]. It will be found, on looking at a map of Japan, that that empire is composed chiefly of four islands, the largest one of which is Niphon; the next in size, Yesso, at the north; and the two smaller ones, Sikok and Kiusiu, at the south. The Commodore had determined to push his way as near as possible to Yedo, the capital, situated at the head of the bay of the same name, so he boldly steamed where steamer had never ventured before, and was soon plowing the remote

9. "Entering the Bay at Yedo." Found in Robert Tomes, *The Americans in Japan: An Abridgement of the Government Narrative of the U.S. Expedition* (New York: D. Appleton & Co, 1857), pp. 150–160.

waters of Japan, and looking with eager interest upon the novel scene which surrounded him. The bay at the entrance is hardly eight miles in width, but it increases to twelve or more beyond. The bold headlands of the precipitous Cape Sagami rose on the left, and on the right extended irregularly the mountainous district of Awa.

As the ships closed in with the land, and as the fog occasionally lifted, a glance was here and there caught of the neighboring shores that were observed to rise in precipitous bluffs, which connected landward with undulating hills. Deep ravines, green with rich verdure, divided the slopes, and opened into small expanses of alluvial land, washed by the waters of the bay into the form of inlets, about the borders of which were grouped various Japanese villages. The uplands were beautifully varied with cultivated fields and tufted woods; while far behind rose the mountains, height upon height, in the inland distance.

The shores of the bay, particularly on the western side, were populous with a succession of towns and villages, picturesquely grouped in groves of pine and other trees. The rising ground which came down from the mountainous interior, abruptly terminated at the water's edge in precipitous headlands, which were crowned with white forts, more formidable in appearance than in reality. The bay was busy with trading-junks, sailing up and down with their broad sails, or putting in here and there at the various ports.

The fleet of Japanese boats, supposed to be government vessels, pulled out into the stream, with the apparent purpose of arresting the progress of the squadron. The steamers, however, passed them contemptuously by, and as they moved along rapidly on their course, at the rate of eight or nine knots an hour, with all their sails furled, the Japanese were soon left behind, and in a state, evidently, of much amazement at the sight of the first vessels they had ever beheld impelled by steam. As the day advanced the sun came out, dispelling the mist which had gathered over the land, and revealing a wide prospect of the distant country. Mount Fuzi [Fuji] was now seen rising to an immense height, with its cone-like summit covered with snow, which glistened brightly in the sun.

The ships, as they approached their anchorage, continued sounding at every turn of the steamers' wheels, and they moved on slowly and cautiously until they reached a part of the bay off the city of Uraga, on the western side. The anchors were now let go, and the squadron was securely moored in Japanese waters, within a nearer distance of the capital of Yedo than any foreign vessel had ever ventured. As the ships brought to, commanding with their guns the town of Uraga and the battery upon its promontory, two guns were fired from the neighboring forts, and rockets were discharged into the air, for the purpose probably of signalizing the authorities at the capital. An immense fleet of government boats, each distinguished by a white flag at the stern, with a black central stripe and a tassel at the bow, came, in accordance with the usual practice in Japanese waters, hovering about the squadron. The Commodore had issued orders that no one from the shore should be allowed to board either of his vessels, except his own flag-ship. Some of the boats, however, attempted to get alongside the *Saratoga*, and the crews clung to the chains until they were repelled with considerable violence.

One of the Japanese boats was allowed to come alongside of the *Susquehanna*, and everyone on board of the steamer was struck with the resemblance of her build, as well as of the others, to that of the famous yacht *America*. Her bows were sharp, her beam broad, and her stern slightly tapering. She was trimly built, of pine wood apparently, without a touch of paint, and was propelled over the water with great swiftness by a numerous crew of boatmen, who, standing to their oars at the stern, sculled instead of rowing, the boat. The men were naked, with the exception of a cloth about their loins, and were wonder-fully stalwart and active fellows. Two persons, armed each with a couple of swords, a Japanese mark of official rank, stood toward the bows, and were evidently men of authority. As the boat reached the side of the steamer, one of these dignitaries held up a scroll, which turned out to be a document in the French and Dutch languages, ordering off the ships, and forbidding them to anchor at their peril. No notice was taken of this very peremptory summons, and the officer on the deck of the Commodore's ship refused positively to touch the paper.

The chief functionary on the boat made signs to have the gangway let down, that he might come on board the *Susquehanna*. This was reported to the Commodore, who kept secluded in his cabin, and he sent word that no one but a dignitary of the highest rank would be received. The Chinese interpreter attached to the squadron tried to make this understood to the Japanese, but as there seemed some difficulty, one of the two functionaries in the boat, who was the chief spokesman, cried out in very good English, "I can speak Dutch!" The Dutch interpreter was then summoned in the emergency, and a parley ensued, in the course of which it was learned that the two officials alongside were Nagasima Saboroske, the Vice-Governor of Uraga, and Hori Tatsnoske, an interpreter. As they insisted that they were the proper persons with whom to confer, they were admitted on board, and were received in the captain's cabin on deck. The Commodore had resolved, from motives of policy, to keep himself entirely secluded until a personage of the highest rank was appointed to meet him, and accordingly communicated with the visitors only through his subordinate officers. The Japanese were now told that the Commodore bore a letter to the Emperor from the President of the United States, which he was prepared to deliver so soon as a proper person was appointed to receive it. To this they replied that Nagasaki, in the island of Kiusou, was the only place where any such communication could be received, and that the ships must proceed there immediately. This being reported to the Commodore, he sent back an answer declaring that he would not go to Nagasaki; and, moreover, if the authorities did not remove their boats, which were thronging about the ships, he would disperse them by force. This last piece of intelligence produced a very prompt effect, for the Vice-Governor of Uraga rose hurriedly on learning it, and going to the gangway, beckoned the guard-boats away. In reference to the reception of the President's letter, the Japanese dignitary said he had nothing more to say, but that another personage of higher rank would come next morning and confer with the Commodore about it. The Japanese now took their departure.

The presence of the Americans in the bay of Yedo was evidently exciting a very lively apprehension among those on shore, for guns were frequently firing, signal rockets shooting up into the air, soldiers parading about the batteries on the various headlands, and at night bells were tolling and beacon-fires were blazing and illumining the long extent of shore.

In accordance with the Vice-Governor's promise, his superior, the Governor of Uraga, visited the *Susquehanna* next day, notwithstanding the former gentleman had said, at first, that he himself was the proper person, and that it was against the laws of Japan for the latter to board a foreign ship. But this kind of deception is a recognized element of Japanese diplomacy, and lying is an established function of Japanese official duty, so it was considered as a matter of course, and the Commodore regulated his conduct accordingly. The Governor, who sent in his name upon his gigantic red card, as Kayamon Yezaimon, was a more imposing personage than his Vice-Governor, and was robed in character with his greater pretensions. He wore the usual Japanese loose gown, something like a clerical robe, which in his case was of rich silk, embroidered with a pattern of peacock feathers. In the sash which girded his waist were thrust the two swords of dignity, and on his head was a lacquered cap, like a reversed basin, reminding one of Don Quixote's helmet of Mambrino. When he uncovered, the usual manner of dressing the hair was disclosed, in which the head is shaved from the forehead far back, while the locks at the sides and above the neck being allowed to grow to a great length, are drawn up, and, being plastered and anointed with pomatum, are fastened in a knot which is stuck to the bald spot on the top. Yezaimon was admitted to an interview, not, however, with the Commodore, who still preserved his dignified reserve, but with one of his captains. A long conversation ensued, in the course of which he was told very much the same things as had been said to his predecessor. He, finding that the Commodore was resolute in his declaration that he would not go to Nagasaki, promised to refer the subject to the imperial government. Nagasaki, it will be recollected, is the place where the Dutch factory is established, and where the Japanese desire to confine all their relations with foreigners, under the same degrading restrictions as those to which the Hollanders have, for the sake of a little trade, so long and so discreditably submitted.

The Commodore had sent out a number of boats, well-armed, to survey the bay, and as they proceeded in their work, closing in with the land, troops of Japanese soldiers thronged the shores and the batteries, while fleets of government boats, with armed men, under the command of military officers, pushed out into the stream, with the apparent purpose of intercepting the surveyors. The American lieutenant who led the survey party ordered his men to rest upon their oars awhile, and to adjust the caps to their pistols, that they might be prepared for what appeared to be the imminent prospect of a collision. The Japanese, however, observing the resolute attitude of the strangers, sculled their trim boats fast away, and the Americans were left undisturbed in their labors.

Yezaimon having observed the survey boats busy in the bay, expressed great anxiety, and declared that it was against the Japanese laws, to which he was answered that the American laws command it, and that the Americans were as much bound to obey the latter as his countrymen were the former. The Commodore had everything in battle array in case of a rupture; he had cleared the decks, placed his guns in position and shotted them, put the small arms into order, overhauled the ammunition, arranged the sentinels, and had done all that was usual before meeting an enemy. Not that the Commodore anticipated actual hostilities, but that he was resolved to be on the alert in case of an emergency, knowing that the best means of avoiding war was to be well prepared for it.

The Japanese, on their part, were no less engaged in busy preparation, furbishing up their forts and extending long stretches of black canvas to either side, with the view of giving them a more formidable aspect, not conscious apparently that the telescopes from the ships' decks disclosed all their sham contrivances for effect. The Japanese soldiers showed themselves in great force about the batteries, glittering in their gay robes of bright blue and red, while their lacquered caps and tall spears shone brightly in the sun's light. Numbers of government boats also thronged the neighboring shores.

After the most provoking and tedious negotiation with the Governor of Uraga, who almost daily visited the *Susquehanna,* and pertinaciously offered every obstacle in his power to the Commodore's resolute determination to be received by a proper personage to whom he might deliver the President's letter, it was at last reluctantly decided by the Government of Japan that the Commodore's wish should be complied with. Accordingly, Thursday, the 14th of July, 1853, was the day appointed for an interview. It was only by the Commodore's urgent demand, and the threat that he would carry the President's letter to Yedo and deliver it in person, that the authorities were prevailed upon to intermit their tedious and prevaricating diplomacy, and, after a delay of four days, to fix the time for the reception on shore.

"I will wait until Tuesday, the 12th of July, and no longer," were the emphatic words of the Commodore, and on that day the answer of the Emperor came, appointing, as we have seen, the subsequent Thursday for the reception.

Document 8

Letter from Commodore Matthew C. Perry [Sent in Connection with the Delivery of a White Flag] to Unknown Japanese Authorities, July 14, 1853[10]

In the days following the U.S. squadron's arrival at the mouth of Edo Bay, Japanese representatives sought to rebuff the Americans and obfuscate in their talks with Commodore Perry's representatives. These tactics had served the Japanese quite well for several decades in the early nineteenth century when Westerners sought to parley with them. But Commodore Perry refused to submit to this approach. This time he used much stronger language in his interactions with the Japanese. He characterized their unwillingness to talk and normalize diplomatic relations as a moral failure, possibly even transgressive. He threatened violence and made clear that in any conflict, Japan could not succeed. Perry's open threat of force was decisive.

For years several countries have applied for trade, but you have opposed them on account of a national law. You have thus acted against divine principles and your sin cannot be greater than it is. What we say thus does not necessarily mean, as has already been communicated by the Dutch boat, that we expect mutual trade by all means. If you are still to disagree we would then take up arms and inquire into the sin against the divine principles, and you would also make sure of your law and fight in defence. When one considers such an occasion, however, one will realize the victory will naturally be ours and you shall by no means overcome us. If in such a situation you seek for a reconciliation, you should put up the white flag that we have recently presented to you, and we would accordingly stop firing and conclude peace with you, turning our battleships aside.

COMMODORE PERRY

10. *Meiji Japan through Contemporary Sources*, vol. 2, *1844–1882*, compiled and published by the Centre for East Asian Cultural Studies (Tokyo: Toyo Bunko, 1969), pp. 15–16.

Document 9

Letter from Millard Fillmore, President of the United States of America, to His Imperial Majesty, the Emperor of Japan (Written in 1852, Delivered by Commodore Perry in 1853)[11]

The letter by President Millard Fillmore to the shogun (emperor) of Japan contained several requests and one demand. The requests were for trade and a port (or ports) at which U.S. commercial vessels could stop and reprovision. The United States demanded that Japan treat shipwrecked sailors with basic humanity and provide some means for their safe return. The phrase "we are very much in earnest in this" is quite strong in the language of diplomacy and conveyed the seriousness of U.S. demands. It was not an ultimatum, but intimated that stronger measures could result if Japan continued to treat as criminals those U.S. castaways who washed up on its shores.

Great and Good Friend: I send you this public letter by Commodore Matthew C. Perry, an officer of the highest rank in the navy of the United States, and commander of the squadron now visiting your imperial majesty's dominions.

I have directed Commodore Perry to assure your imperial majesty that I entertain the kindest feelings toward your majesty's person and government, and that I have no other object in sending him to Japan but to propose to your imperial majesty that the United States and Japan should live in friendship and have commercial intercourse with each other.

The Constitution and laws of the United States forbid all interference with the religious or political concerns of other nations. I have particularly charged Commodore Perry to abstain from every act which could possibly disturb the tranquility of your imperial majesty's dominions.

11. Letter from President Millard Fillmore to the emperor of Japan. Found in Perry, et al., *Narrative of the Expedition of an American Squadron to the China Seas and Japan*, pp. 296–298.

The United States of America reach from ocean to ocean, and our Territory of Oregon and State of California lie directly opposite to the dominions of your imperial majesty. Our steamships can go from California to Japan in eighteen days.

Our great State of California produces about sixty millions of dollars in gold every year, besides silver, quicksilver, precious stones, and many other valuable articles. Japan is also a rich and fertile country, and produces many very valuable articles. Your imperial majesty's subjects are skilled in many of the arts. I am desirous that our two countries should trade with each other, for the benefit both of Japan and the United States.

We know that the ancient laws of your imperial majesty's government do not allow of foreign trade, except with the Chinese and the Dutch; but as the state of the world changes and new governments are formed, it seems to be wise, from time to time, to make new laws. There was a time when the ancient laws of your imperial majesty's government were first made.

About the same time America, which is sometimes called the New World, was first discovered and settled by the Europeans. For a long time there were but a few people, and they were poor. They have now become quite numerous; their commerce is very extensive; and they think that if your imperial majesty were so far to change the ancient laws as to allow a free trade between the two countries it would be extremely beneficial to both.

If your imperial majesty is not satisfied that it would be safe altogether to abrogate the ancient laws which forbid foreign trade, they might be suspended for five or ten years, so as to try the experiment. If it does not prove as beneficial as was hoped, the ancient laws can be restored. The United States often limit their treaties with foreign States to a few years, and then renew them or not, as they please.

I have directed Commodore Perry to mention another thing to your imperial majesty. Many of our ships pass every year from California to China; and great numbers of our people pursue the whale fishery near the shores of Japan. It sometimes happens, in stormy weather, that one of our ships is wrecked on your imperial majesty's shores. In all such cases we ask, and expect, that our unfortunate people should be treated with kindness, and that their property should be protected, till we can send a vessel and bring them away. We are very much in earnest in this.

Commodore Perry is also directed by me to represent to your imperial majesty that we understand there is a great abundance of coal and provisions in the Empire of Japan. Our steamships, in crossing the great ocean, burn a great deal of coal, and it is not convenient to bring it all the way from America. We wish that our steamships and other vessels should be allowed to stop in Japan and supply themselves with coal, provisions, and water. They will pay for them in money, or anything else your imperial majesty's subjects may prefer; and we request your imperial majesty to appoint a convenient port, in the southern part of the Empire, where our vessels may stop for this purpose. We are very desirous of this.

These are the only objects for which I have sent Commodore Perry, with a powerful squadron, to pay a visit to your imperial majesty's renowned city of Yedo [Edo/Tokyo]: friendship, commerce, a supply of coal and provisions, and protection for our shipwrecked people.

We have directed Commodore Perry to beg your imperial majesty's acceptance of a few presents. They are of no great value in themselves; but some of them may serve as specimens of the articles manufactured in the United States, and they are intended as tokens of our sincere and respectful friendship.

May the Almighty have your imperial majesty in His great and holy keeping!

In witness whereof, I have caused the great seal of the United States to be hereunto affixed, and have subscribed the same with my name, at the city of Washington, in America, the seat of my government, on the thirteenth day of the month of November, in the year one thousand eight hundred and fifty-two.

[Seal attached]

Your good friend,
MILLARD FILLMORE

By the President:

Edward Everett,
Secretary of State.

Document 10

Letter from Commodore Matthew C. Perry to the Emperor of Japan (1853)[12]

In addition to the letter from U.S. President Millard Fillmore to the shogun (emperor) of Japan, Commodore Perry also penned a note to the shogun. In this letter, Perry expanded and provided context on President Fillmore's letter. In contrast to the president's letter, Perry's articulated the threat posed by the United States if Japan continued its policy toward shipwrecked sailors. He stated that there could be no friendly relations between the two countries if conditions persisted in their (then) present condition. He made clear that there would be military action unless Japan changed its policy. In this correspondence, Perry wanted there to be absolutely no possibility of a misunderstanding regarding U.S. intentions toward the Japanese.

Commodore Perry to the Emperor.
United States Steam Frigate *Susquehanna*,
Off the Coast of Japan, July 7, 1853

The undersigned, commander-in-chief of all the naval forces of the United States of America stationed in the East India, China, and Japan seas, has been sent by his government of this country, on a friendly mission, with ample powers to negotiate with the government of Japan, touching certain matters which have been fully set forth in the letter of the President of the United States, copies of which, together with copies of the letter of credence of the undersigned, in the English, Dutch, and Chinese languages, are herewith transmitted.

The original of the President's letter, and of the letter of credence, prepared in a manner suited to the exalted station of your imperial majesty, will be presented by the undersigned in person, when it may please your majesty to appoint a day for his reception.

12. Letter from Commodore Perry to the emperor. Found in Perry, et al., *Narrative of the Expedition of an American Squadron to the China Seas and Japan*, pp. 299–300.

The undersigned has been commanded to state that the President entertains the most friendly feelings towards Japan, but has been surprised and grieved to learn that when any of the people of the United States go, of their own accord, or are thrown by the perils of the sea, within the dominations of your imperial majesty, they are treated as if they were your worst enemies.

The undersigned refers to the cases of the American ships *Morrison*, *Lagoda*, and *Lawrence*.

With the Americans, as indeed with all Christian people, it is considered a sacred duty to receive with kindness, and to succor and protect all, of whatever nation, who may be cast upon their shores, and such has been the course of the Americans with respect to all Japanese subjects who have fallen under their protection.

The government of the United States desires to obtain from that of Japan some positive assurance that persons who may hereafter be shipwrecked on the coast of Japan, or driven by stress of weather into her ports, shall be treated with humanity.

The undersigned is commanded to explain to the Japanese that the United States are connected with no government in Europe, and that their laws do not interfere with the religion of their own citizens, much less with that of other nations.

That they inhabit a great country which lies directly between Japan and Europe, and which was discovered by the nations of Europe about the same time that Japan herself was first visited by Europeans; that the portion of the American continent lying nearest to Europe was first settled by emigrants from that part of the world; that its population has rapidly spread through the country, until it has reached the shores of the Pacific Ocean; that we have now large cities, from which, with the aid of steam vessels, we can reach Japan in eighteen or twenty days; that our commerce with all this region of the globe is rapidly increasing, and the Japan seas will soon be covered with our vessels.

Therefore, as the United States and Japan are becoming every day nearer and nearer to each other, the President desires to live in peace and friendship with your imperial majesty, but no friendship can long exist, unless Japan ceases to act towards Americans as if they were her enemies.

However wise this policy may originally have been, it is unwise and impracticable now that the intercourse between the two countries is so much more easy and rapid than it formerly was.

The undersigned holds out all these arguments in the hope that the Japanese government will see the necessity of averting unfriendly collision between the two nations, by responding favorably to the propositions of amity, which are now made in all sincerity.

Many of the large ships-of-war destined to visit Japan have not yet arrived in these seas, though they are hourly expected; and the undersigned, as an evidence of his friendly intentions, has brought but four of the smaller ones, designing, should it become necessary, to return to Edo in the ensuing spring with a much larger force.

But it is expected that the government of your imperial majesty will render such return unnecessary, by acceding at once to the very reasonable and pacific overtures contained in the President's letter, and which will be further explained by the undersigned on the first fitting occasion.

With the most profound respect for your imperial majesty, and entertaining a sincere hope that you may long live to enjoy health and happiness, the undersigned subscribes himself,

M. C. Perry,
Commander-in-chief of the United States Naval Forces
in the East India, China, and Japan seas.

To His Imperial Majesty,
The Emperor of Japan

Document 11

Treaty of Kanagawa, March 31, 1854[13]

The treaty below was the first signed by the Japanese government with a foreign power (other than the Dutch) in more than two centuries. It was signed under extreme duress and the threat of military action. The primary objective of the United States regarding shipwrecked sailors and the approval of limited trading opportunities had been satisfied in this agreement. The Japanese, understandably, were not practiced in the art of diplomacy and likely didn't consider all of the ramifications of the agreement. In particular, they appeared to be unaware that they had also agreed to the exchange of consuls and were surprised when the first U.S. consul, Townsend Harris, arrived to take up his post. In addition, the "most favored nation" clause in the agreement meant that the United States would enjoy any rights and privileges other nations subsequently wrangled out of the Japanese in their treaties. This meant that there would be continuous addenda to this agreement.

THE UNITED STATES of America and the Empire of Japan, desiring to establish firm, lasting, and sincere friendship between the two nations, have resolved to fix, in a manner clear and positive, by means of a treaty or general convention of peace and amity, the rules which shall in future be mutually observed in the intercourse of their respective countries; for which most desirable object the President of the United States has conferred full powers on his Commissioner, Matthew Calbraith Perry, Special Ambassador of the United States to Japan, and the August Sovereign of Japan has given similar full powers to his Commissioners Hayashi-Daigaku-nokami, Ido, Prince of Tsus-Sima; Izawa, Prince of Mimasaki; and Udono, member of the Board of Revenue.

And the said Commissioners, after having exchanged their said full powers, and duly considered the premises, have agreed to the following articles:

13. Letter from Commodore Perry to the emperor. Found in Perry, et al., *Narrative of the Expedition of an American Squadron to the China Seas and Japan*, pp. 440–442.

ARTICLE I

There shall be a perfect, permanent, and universal peace, and a sincere and cordial amity between the United States of America on the one part, and the Empire of Japan on the other part, and between their people respectively, without exception of persons or places.

ARTICLE II

The port of Simoda, in the principality of Idzu, and the port of Hakodadi, in the principality of Matsmai, are granted by the Japanese as ports for the reception of American ships, where they can be supplied with wood, water, provisions, and coal, and other articles their necessities may require, as far as the Japanese have them. The time for opening the first-named port is immediately on signing this treaty; the last-named port is to be opened immediately after the same day in the ensuing Japanese year.

NOTE.—A tariff of prices shall be given by the Japanese officers of the things which they can furnish, payment for which shall be made in gold and silver coin.

ARTICLE III

Whenever ships of the United States are thrown or wrecked on the coast of Japan, the Japanese vessels will assist them, and carry their crews to Simoda, or Hakodadi, and hand them over to their countrymen, appointed to receive them; whatever articles the shipwrecked men may have preserved shall likewise be restored, and the expenses incurred in the rescue and support of Americans and Japanese who may thus be thrown upon the shores of either nation are not to be refunded.

ARTICLE IV

Those shipwrecked persons and other citizens of the United States shall be free as in other countries, and not subjected to confinement, but shall be amenable to just laws.

ARTICLE V

Shipwrecked men and other citizens of the United States, temporarily living at Simoda and Hakodadi, shall not be subject to such restrictions and confinement as the Dutch and Chinese are at Nagasaki, but shall be free at Simoda to go where they please within the limits of seven Japanese miles from a small island in the harbor of Simoda marked on the accompanying chart hereto appended; and shall in like manner be free to go where they please at Hakodadi, within limits to be defined after the visit of the United States squadron to that place.

ARTICLE VI

If there be any other sort of goods wanted, or any business which shall require to be arranged, there shall be careful deliberation between the parties in order to settle such matters.

ARTICLE VII

It is agreed that ships of the United States resorting to the ports open to them shall be permitted to exchange gold and silver coin and articles of goods for other articles of goods, under such regulations as shall be temporarily established by the Japanese Government for that purpose. It is stipulated, however, that the ships of the United States shall be permitted to carry away whatever articles they are unwilling to exchange.

ARTICLE VIII

Wood, water, provisions, coal, and goods required, shall only be procured through the agency of Japanese officers appointed for that purpose, and in no other manner.

ARTICLE IX

It is agreed that if at any future day the Government of Japan shall grant to any other nation or nations privileges and advantages which are not herein granted to the United States and the citizens thereof, that these same privileges and advantages shall be granted likewise to the United States and to the citizens thereof, without any consultation or delay.

ARTICLE X

Ships of the United States shall be permitted to resort to no other ports in Japan but Simoda and Hakodadi, unless in distress or forced by stress of weather.

ARTICLE XI

There shall be appointed, by the Government of the United States, Consuls or Agents to reside in Simoda, at any time after the expiration of eighteen months from the date of the signing of this treaty, provided that either of the two Governments deem such arrangement necessary.

ARTICLE XII

The present convention having been concluded and duly signed, shall be obligatory and faithfully observed by the United States of America and Japan, and by the citizens and subjects of each respective Power; and it is to be ratified and approved by the President of the United States, by and with the advice and consent of the Senate thereof, and by the August Sovereign of Japan, and the ratification shall be exchanged within eighteen months from the date of the signature thereof, or sooner if practicable.

In faith whereof we, the respective Plenipotentiaries of the United States of America and the Empire of Japan aforesaid, have signed and sealed these presents.

Done at Kanagawa, this thirty-first day of March, in the year of our Lord Jesus Christ one thousand eight hundred and fifty-four and of Kayei the seventh year, third month and third day.

M. C. PERRY.

(HERE FOLLOW THE SIGNATURES OF THE JAPANESE)

Document 12

Japanese Map of the World (1850s)[14]

The map below demonstrates that even though Japan had secluded itself from the rest of the world during most of the Tokugawa period (1600–1868), its leaders had a thorough and sophisticated understanding of the geopolitical situation around the world. Most of the countries in this image of the world are noted, along with rudimentary political boundaries and major cities. Even North America is detailed with major rivers, cities, and people groups. It is not known how the Tokugawa used this information to formulate policy or the extent to which the average Japanese might have known about the outside world. But it is clear that Japan was able to keep abreast of changes in the world as the Tokugawa period was coming to a close.

14. *Sekai zu* (World Map), map published near the end of the Tokugawa period. Publisher unknown. Found in David Rumsey Map Collection website, Japanese historical maps, accessed February 6, 2019, http://japanmaps.davidrumsey.com.

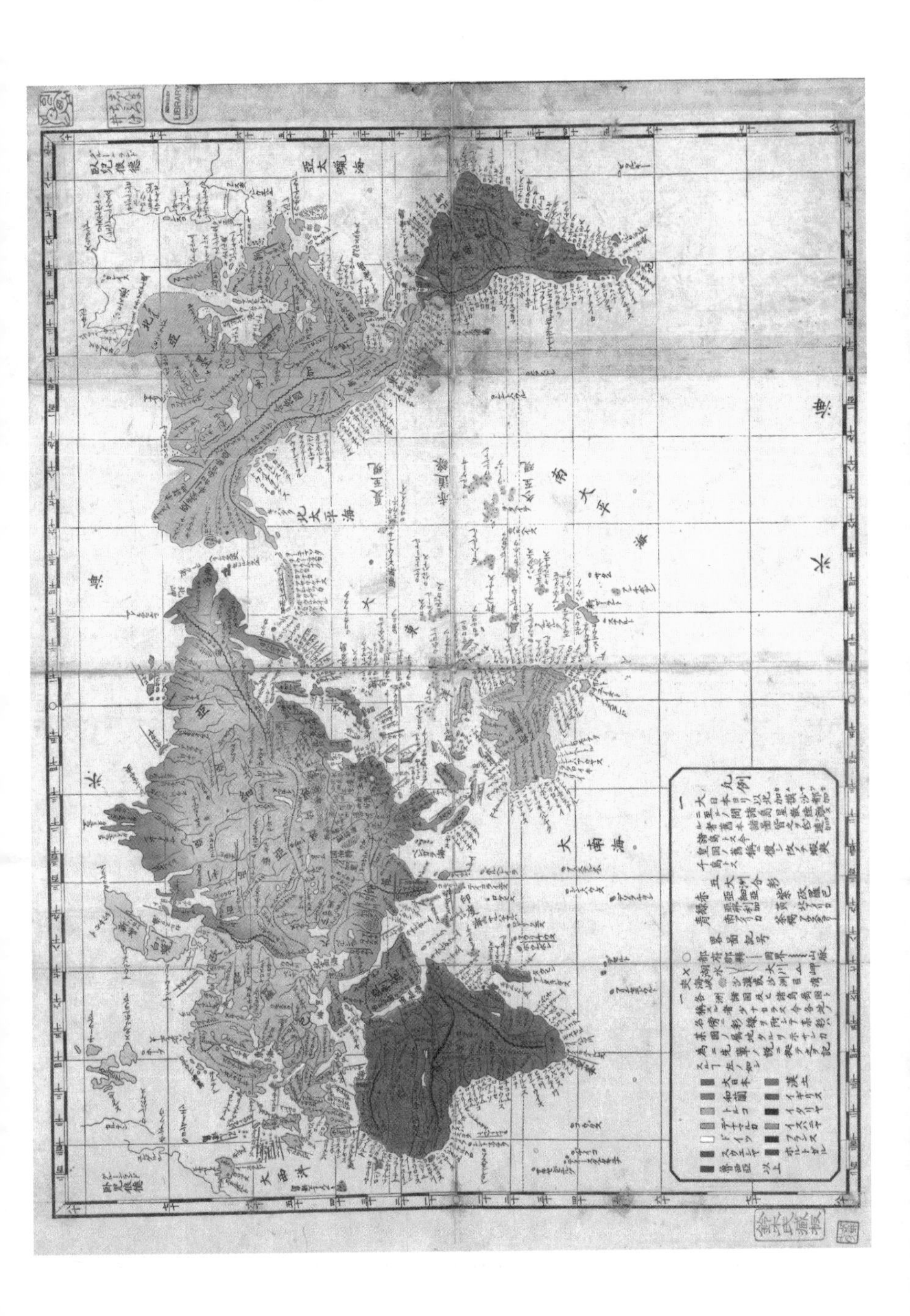

Document 13

Commodore Perry's Fleet as Depicted in an 1853 Woodblock Print[15]

This print provides perspective on how the Japanese viewed the ceremonial meeting of Commodore Perry and Japanese officials. Note that the ships are depicted as black, and two of them are clearly paddlewheel vessels. The steam-driven vessels are spewing smoke. Though the image is stylized and not drawn to scale, it gives a sense of the size of the U.S. vessels and the potential threat they posed to the coast of Japan.

15. Commodore Perry's Fleet as depicted in an 1853 woodblock print. From the 横浜市立図書館 (Yokohama City Public Library collection).

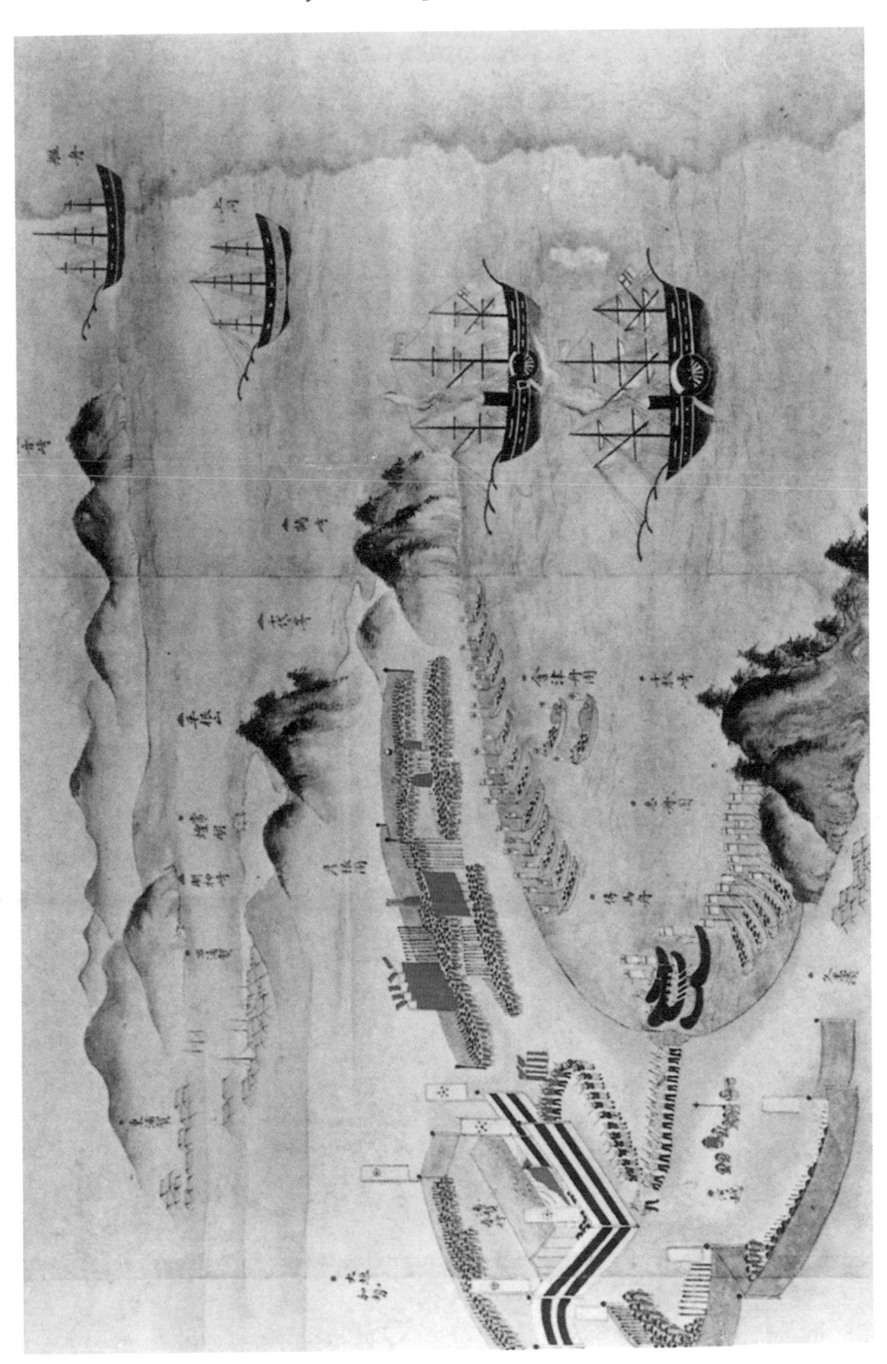

Document 14

A U.S.-Produced Lithograph of the Meeting between Commodore Perry and the Japanese in 1853[16]

This view of the famous meeting provides a clear contrast to the previous image. Whereas the Japanese image illustrated the threat posed by the presence of the United States, the U.S. version shows how vulnerable but nonetheless dignified the U.S. delegation was during the ceremonial landing. The U.S. delegation is clearly surrounded and outnumbered.

16. *First Landing at Gorahama,* by W. Heine. Digitized image found at the U.S. Library of Congress.

FIRST LANDING AT GORAHAMA.

Document 15

Japanese Woodblock Print of Commodore Perry at Sixty Years Old (1854)[17]

The Japanese were extremely interested in the physical appearance of Westerners and, in particular, of Commodore Perry. This portrait, the work of an unknown artist, is one of the more lifelike ones produced during the period. As usual, Perry is portrayed as hirsute, with a long pointed nose and dour countenance. The artist also shows wrinkles and takes great pains to mention that he is about sixty years old, the age in the Chinese system at which one is to be revered for longevity and wisdom.

17. *Ikoku Ochibe Kago* [A Basket of Fallen Leaves from a Foreign Country] (Tokyo: Bigakudo, 1854).

寅六十才
提督ペルリ省像

Document 16

On Coastal Defense (1853)[18]

In the passage below, one of Japan's most powerful daimyō *offers his thoughts on the best way to respond to U.S. demands. Tokugawa Nariaki (1800–1860) was* daimyō *of Mito domain, father of the last shogun, and an influential leader in the Meiji Restoration. His admonition on the use of force and militaristic posture were adopted by other provocateurs of the era. Though unaware of just how weak Japan's military position was, he seemed prescient about the possible collapse of support for the Tokugawa government if they signed an agreement with the United States.*

It is my belief that the first and most urgent of our tasks is for the *bakufu* to make its choice between peace and war, and having determined its policy to pursue it unwaveringly thereafter. When we consider the respective advantages and disadvantages of war and peace, we find that if we put our trust in war the whole country's morale will be increased and even if we sustain an initial defeat we will in the end expel the foreigner; while if we put our trust in peace, even though things may seem tranquil for a time, the morale of the country will be greatly lowered and we will come in the end to complete collapse. This has been amply demonstrated in the history of China and is a fact that men of intelligence, both past and present, have always known. It is therefore unnecessary for me to speak of this in detail. However, I propose to give here in outline the ten reasons why in my view we must never choose the policy of peace.

1. Although our country's territory is not extensive, foreigners both fear and respect us. That, after all, is because our resoluteness and military prowess have been clearly demonstrated to the world outside by such events as the conquest of Korea by the Empress Jingō in very ancient times; by the repulse of the Mongols in the Kōan period (1278–1288)

18. "Tokugawa Nariaki to the Japanese Government: Observations of Coast Defense." Found in *Dai Nihon Komonjo: Bakumatsu Gaikoku Kankei Monjo* [Ancient Records from Imperial Japan: Documents Related to Foreign Counties in the Bakumatsu Period] (Tokyo: Tokyo University Shuppankai, 1972), pp. 509–522. Translation by W. G. Beasley, *Select Documents on Japanese Foreign Policy, 1853–1868* (Oxford: Oxford University Press, 1955), pp. 102–107.

during the middle ages; and in the recent past by the invasion of Korea in the Bunroku period (1592–1596) and the suppression of Christianity in the Keichō (1596–1615) and Kanei (1624–1644) periods. Despite this, the Americans who arrived recently, though fully aware of the *bakufu*'s prohibition, entered Uraga displaying a white flag as a symbol of peace and insisted on presenting their written requests. Moreover they entered Edo Bay, fired heavy guns in salute and even went so far as to conduct surveys without permission. They were arrogant and discourteous, their actions an outrage. Indeed, this was the greatest disgrace we have suffered since the dawn of our history. The saying is that if the enemy dictates terms in one's own capital, one's country is disgraced. The foreigners having thus ignored our prohibition and penetrated our waters even to the vicinity of the capital, threatening us and making demands upon us, should it happen not only that the *bakufu* fails to expel them but also that it concludes an agreement in accordance with their requests, then I fear it would be impossible to maintain our national prestige. That is the first reason we must never choose the policy of peace.

2. The prohibition of Christianity is the first rule of the Tokugawa house. Public notices concerning it are posted everywhere, even to the remotest corner of every province. It is said that even so, during the Bunsei period (1818–1830), men have been executed for propagating this religion secretly in Osaka. The *bakufu* can never ignore or overlook the evils of Christianity. Yet if the Americans are allowed to come again this religion will inevitably raise its head once more, however strict the prohibition; and this, I fear, is something we could never justify to the spirits of our ancestors. That is the second reason why we must never choose the policy of peace.

3. To exchange our valuable articles like gold, silver, copper, and iron for useless foreign goods like woollens and satin is to incur great loss while acquiring not the smallest benefit. The best course of all would be for the *bakufu* to put a stop to the trade with Holland. By contrast, to open such valueless trade with others besides the Dutch would, I believe, inflict the greatest possible harm to our country. That is the third reason why we must never choose the policy of peace.

4. For some years Russia, England, and others have sought trade with us, but the *bakufu* has not permitted it. Should permission be granted to the Americans, on what grounds would it be possible to refuse if Russia and the others [again] request it? This is the fourth reason why we must never choose the policy of peace.

5. It is widely stated that [apart from trade] the foreigners have no other evil designs and that if only the *bakufu* will permit trade there will be no further difficulty. However, it is their practice first to seek a foothold by means of trade and then to go on to propagate Christianity and make other unreasonable demands. Thus we would be repeating the blunders of others, seen remotely in the Christianity incidents of the Kanei period (1624–1644) and before [in Japan] and more recently in the Opium War in China. That is the fifth reason why we must never choose the policy of peace.

6. Though the Rangakusha group may argue secretly that world conditions are much changed from what they were, Japan alone clinging to the ideas of seclusion in isolation amidst the seas, that this is a constant source of danger to us and that our best course would therefore be to communicate with foreign countries and open an extensive trade; yet, to my mind, if the people of Japan stand firmly united, if we complete our military preparations and return to the state of society that existed before the middle ages, then we will even be able to go out against foreign countries and spread abroad our fame and prestige. But if we open trade at the demand of the foreigners, for no better reason than that, our habits today being those of peace and indolence, men have shown fear merely at the coming of a handful of foreign warships, then it would truly be a vain illusion to think of evolving any long-range plan for going out against foreign countries. That is the sixth reason why we must never choose the policy of peace.

7. The *bakufu* entrusted the defense of the Uraga district to the Hikone and Wakamatsu fiefs, and I hear that the Aizu retainers [from Wakamatsu] have already gone there travelling night and day for some 170 miles or more despite the heat. I also hear that in addition to this the *daimyō* ordered to defend Edo Bay are sending troops at once. All this is admirable. But if we ignore the fact that the foreigners went so far as to enter Edo Bay and carry out surveys without permission, if we do not take action and expel them, this will be to allow the men of all provinces to exhaust themselves in activity that is but vain and wasted effort, and in the end our people will be brought to a state of complete collapse. That is the seventh reason why we must never choose the policy of peace.

8. When Kuroda and Nabeshima were made responsible for the coast defense of Nagasaki it was not intended that this be directed solely against the Dutch and Chinese. It was a measure directed against all foreigners. But by agreeing to receive written requests from the foreigners at Uraga—and still more were the *bakufu* to conclude an agreement there in accordance with those requests—would we not, as it were, be allowing

the foreigners to enter by the back door, thus rendering futile the guard duties entrusted to those two families and arousing their resentment? That is the eighth reason why we must never choose the policy of peace.

9. I hear that all, even though they be commoners, who have witnessed the recent actions of the foreigners, think them abominable; and if the *bakufu* does not expel these insolent foreigners root and branch there may be some who will complain in secret, asking to what purpose have been all the preparations of gun-emplacements. It is inevitable that men should think in this way when they have seen how arrogantly the foreigners acted at Uraga. That, I believe, is because even the humblest are conscious of the debt they owe their country, and it is indeed a promising sign. Since even ignorant commoners are talking in this way, I fear that if the *bakufu* does not decide to carry out expulsion, if its handling of the matter shows nothing but excess of leniency and appeasement of the foreigners, then the lower orders may fail to understand its ideas and hence opposition might arise from evil men who had lost their respect for *bakufu* authority. It might even be that *bakufu* control of the great lords would itself be endangered. That is the ninth reason why we must never choose the policy of peace.

10. There are those who say that since the expulsion of foreigners is the ancient law of the Shōgun's ancestors, reissued and reaffirmed in the Bunsei period, the Bakufu has in fact always been firmly resolved to fight, but that even so one must recognize that peace has now lasted so long our armaments are inadequate, and one cannot therefore tell what harm might be done if we too recklessly arouse the anger of the foreigners. In that event, they say, the *bakufu* would be forced to conclude a peace settlement and so its prestige would suffer still further damage. Hence [it is argued], the *bakufu* should show itself compliant at this time and should placate the foreigners, meanwhile exerting all its efforts in military preparations, so that when these preparations have been completed it can more strictly enforce the ancient laws. This argument sounds reasonable enough. However, to my mind the people here [in Edo] are temporizing and half-hearted; and even though the Shōgun exhorts them day and night he cannot make them resolute. Now there is not the slightest chance that the feudal lords will complete military preparations, however many years may pass, unless they are set an example in military matters by the *bakufu*. There have already been clashes in Ezo [Hokkaidō] during the Kansei [1789–1801] and Bunka [1804–1818] periods, but despite the *bakufu*'s efforts to effect military preparations they have not yet been completed. Again, relaxation of the expulsion laws was ordered in 1842,

with the apparent object of first placating the foreigners and then using the respite to complete military preparations, but here, too, I do not think the various lords have made any particular progress in rearming in the twelve years that have since elapsed. On the arrival of the foreign ships recently, all fell into a panic. Some take matters very seriously while foreign ships are actually at anchor here, but once the ships leave and orders are given for them to revert to normal, they all relax once more into idleness and immediately disperse the military equipment which they have hurriedly assembled. It is just as if, regardless of a fire burning beneath the floor of one's house, one neglected all fire-fighting precautions. Indeed, it shows a shameful spirit. I therefore believe that if there be any sign of the *bakufu* pursuing the policy of peace, morale will never rise though preparations made will accordingly be so much ornament, never put to effective use. But if the *bakufu*, now and henceforward, shows itself resolute for expulsion, the immediate effect will be to increase ten-fold the morale of the country and to bring about the completion of military preparations without even the necessity for issuing orders. Hesitant as I am to say so, only by so doing will the Shōgun be able to fulfill his "barbarian-expelling" duty and unite the men of every province in carrying out their proper military functions. That is the tenth reason why we must never choose the policy of peace, and it is by far the most urgent and important of them all.

I have tried to explain above in general terms the relative advantages and disadvantages of the war and peace policies. However, the [policy I recommend] is something that it is easy to understand but difficult to carry out. In these feeble days men tend to cling to peace; they are not fond of defending their country by war. They slander those of us who are determined to fight, calling us lovers of war, men who enjoy conflict. If matters become desperate they might, in their enormous folly, try to overthrow those of us who are determined to fight, offering excuses to the enemy and concluding a peace agreement with him. They would thus in the end bring total destruction upon us. In view of our country's tradition of military courage, however, it is probable that once the *bakufu* has taken a firm decision we shall find no such cowards among us. But good advice is as hard to accept as good medicine is unpleasing to the palate. A temporizing and time-serving policy is the one easiest for men to adopt. It is therefore my belief that in this question of coast defense it is of the first importance that the *bakufu* pay heed [to these matters] and that having once reached a decision it should never waver from it thereafter. . . .

Document 17

Memorial on Foreign Intercourse Presented to the Shogunate by Ii Kamon no Kami (Ii Naosuke) in 1853[19]

The passage below was written by Ii Naosuke (1815–1860), one of the most capable government leaders in the last years of the Tokugawa period. He was a canny politician, farsighted, shrewd, and merciless when dealing with his political rivals. Ii even issued the order to execute Yoshida Shōin in 1859 when he occupied the position of tairō *(great elder). Ii understood better than most Japan's weak military situation in the 1850s. He first wanted to strengthen and unify Japan and then to confront the foreigners later. He recognized that the* sonnō jōi *movement, led by radical samurai largely from Chōshū, Satsuma, and Mito domains, posed an existential threat to the Tokugawa. This prognosis proved correct. However, strong leaders also create strong enemies, and he was assassinated outside the gates of the shogun's palace in 1860. After his death, no Tokugawa leader proved capable of meeting the challenge posed by the radical samurai of the* sonnō jōi *movement.*

Before the year 1636 there were nine government vessels of war, but at that date, owing to the prohibition of Christianity during the rule of Iemitsu, these vessels were stopped from making voyages, and a law was passed closing the seas to navigation, and shutting up the country, trade being permitted only with the Chinese and Dutch. Looking carefully at the circumstances of today, distinguished and far-seeing scholars, who are solicitous for the country's welfare, are discussing the question eagerly. Should a crisis occur now, I do not think that the peace of the country and the safety of the State can be assured by simply maintaining the old laws and closing the seas to navigation of our vessels, and in any case, some time must elapse before measures for defense are complete. Since the destruction of all war vessels of 500 *koku* and over, we have no warships which could use heavy guns in a fight with foreigners. If

19. "Ii Naosuke to bakufu, October 1, 1853"; taken from *Kaikoku Shimatsu* ("The Affair of Opening of the Country"). Found in John Harrington Gubbins, *The Progress of Japan, 1853–1871* (Oxford: Oxford University Press, 1912), pp. 285–288.

they were to obtain a foothold by seizing the Hachijō Islands or Ōshima (Vries Island), we could not let the matter rest there, but without warships I feel uneasy with regard to any scheme for pursuing and attacking them. There is a saying handed down from the past that if the bridge of a besieged castle be taken away it cannot hold out forever; that if two armies are fighting with a river between them the one that crosses and attacks the other will win. It is an old axiom that the advantage is with the side which attacks, and not with that which defends. Our ancestors passed a law closing the ocean to navigation by our ships, but they left a Chinese and Dutch bridge. The bridge will now be convenient to the government in carrying out its foreign policy. If we postpone hostilities for the present, a scheme to obtain certain victory and complete security may be devised. Coal which America desires, is said to be abundant in Kyūshū, and although it has been stated, for reasons of policy, that it is required for use in Japan, if the Americans need it at sea in a sudden emergency, they will come to Nagasaki and ask for it. And if there is a surplus (not wanted by us), it should be given them; firewood and water, too, are things which we should not grudge. With regard to provisions, there are plentiful and scarce years in all countries (and in the former stores ought to be accumulated to provide for the latter), but these ought to be given to shipwrecked people. Moreover, with regard to castaways, these should be cared for, and restored to their homes, as has been done of late years; there is no necessity to examine especially into these cases; communications with regard to all such matters can be made through the Dutch. Again, with regard to trade, there is a national prohibition, but there is a difference between the past and the present; to exchange what one has for what one has not is the law of the universe.

After informing the spirits of our ancestors (of our intentions) we should send merchant vessels from Japan to the trading emporium of the Dutch Company in Java, and selling things to the Americans and Russians carry on trade with them through the medium of the Dutch. It is said that the building of big vessels for navigating the ocean will of course take one or two years. If the Government deals with them (the Americans and Russians) on the same general lines on which it has dealt with the Dutch, they will in this way be taken by surprise. Then we must restore the Government vessels which existed in and before the period of Kwanyei (1624–1644). Orders should be given to the rich merchants of Osaka, Hyōgo, or Sakai, and, shares being given them in the enterprise, strong and big men-of-war and steamers should be built. (In these latter) goods not wanted by Japan should be loaded; Dutchmen should, for a time, be engaged as captains and sailors, honest and capable men should be placed on board, and they should be made to learn how to work the guns, how to navigate the vessel, and how to manage the compass. The vessels should be professedly merchant ships, but in reality no effort should be spared to obtain efficiency in naval drill; the number of these ships should be gradually increased, and at the same time naval training should gradually be perfected, so that Japanese might eventually navigate the high seas independently and, no longer needing the secret information supplied by the Dutch, see directly for themselves the condition of foreign countries; later on, complete naval preparations might be made, and the panic and apprehensions which have hitherto prevailed would be dispelled, the evil of luxury and extravagance be put an end to, and the internal condition of the country as regards military preparation being entirely satisfactory, we should be in a condition to display our martial vigor abroad. Thus, no longer should we remain excluded from the world, but, being completely equipped at home and abroad, the Imperial land (Empire) would be secure. This is my view. Let us go forward (to meet difficulties—not wait for them to come to us) and set to work at once. Having done this, the Government can, in accordance with circumstances, at any time prohibit intercourse as in the Kwanyei period and prevent foreigners from coming to Japan. This is, I think, a good plan. Again with regard to the prohibition of the strange teaching, this should be maintained with the utmost strictness. I understand that it is only of recent years that the Americans and Russians have become fully skilled in the art of navigation. Japanese are naturally skillful and quick, and if they are from this time forward trained, they will surpass foreigners. If, consideration being given to the condition of the country, and the circumstances of the times, the state be guarded securely forever without danger to the Empire from foreign barbarians, even if some alterations be made in the country's ancient laws, the gods will, I think, not disapprove. The point of first importance in the action now to be taken by the Government is, in my opinion, that truth and righteousness should be secured internally. Therefore I am of the opinion that in the first place, a communication should be made to the Court, and Imperial messengers being sent to (the shrines at) Ise, Kiyomizu, and Kagoshima, and a Shōgun's representative to Nikkō, an announcement should be made of the decision to be arrived at by the Government for the tranquility of the country and the security of the state, and the matter left to the will of the gods, and that in this way measures should be taken to bring into agreement the ancient laws of the country of the gods and the wishes of the people.

It is now by no means an easy matter by means of military dispositions in the seas adjacent to the seat of Government to arrange for everything to be in readiness to meet a sudden and unexpected crisis. There should, therefore, not be an instant's delay. However many rings of iron walls may be erected, if foreign complications occur, national harmony cannot be maintained. In any case what is now of pressing importance is that the Government should arrive at a decision for tranquillizing the whole country, and that the necessary orders should be issued to those concerned.

The above views being contrary to the august prohibition, I feel alarmed at putting them forward, but I offer this opinion because we are asked to speak fully, and place our plans, if we have any, before the Government.

Ii Kamon no Kami

Document 18

One Letter to the Shogunate from the Major *Daimyō* in Response to U.S. Demands (1853)[20]

The shogun of Japan died unexpectedly within weeks of Commodore Perry's arrival in 1853. Abe Masahiro (1819–1857), the shogun's senior counselor, understood himself to be a caretaker only, lacking the moral and temporal authority vested in the office of shogun. Nonetheless, he was faced with the unenviable task of rallying the great daimyō *to support the government because some had long-standing grievances against the Tokugawa. As is the Japanese way, Abe wanted to develop consensus on an issue of this importance and queried the great* daimyō *about how best to proceed. Many had not been seriously consulted in decades. It is therefore no surprise that they did not agree on a way forward. Not only was no consensus created, Abe's poll of the* daimyō *revealed a chasm between what Abe believed to be prudent and what many of the great* daimyō *suggested.*

Below is one response to Abe's query. It is an example of one of the more thoughtful positions taken by the daimyō*. The author (unknown) suggests neither immediate military action nor the immediate opening of the country. But he is nonetheless unyielding and suggests stalling as long as possible until the country has made adequate preparations for defense.*

Of these matters [raised by the Americans], the question of kind treatment for castaways was settled by the *bakufu* orders of 1842. Hence demanding it now may well be a subterfuge by which the Americans hope to find justification and pretext for such action as will force compliance with the [other] demands, a plan by which they may obtain a foothold. We must certainly tell them that the *bakufu* has already made

20. "Jisha-bugyō, machi-bugyō and kanjō bugyō to Rōjū; memorandum concerning the American letters, submitted to Abe Masahiro on August 26, 1853." Found in *Dai Nihon Komonjo: Bakumatsu Gaikoku Kankei Monjo* [Ancient Records from Imperial Japan: Documents Related to Foreign Counties in the Bakumatsu Period] (Tokyo: Tokyo University Shuppankai, 1972), pp. 606–612. Translation by Beasley, *Select Documents on Japanese Foreign Policy, 1853–1868*, pp. 107–112.

a pronouncement on this subject. For the rest, it is quite impossible for the *bakufu* to agree to appoint a port at which they may be supplied with coal, food, and so on—to say nothing of such questions as friendship and trade. Previous to this, there have already been requests for trade from various Western peoples, but on each occasion the *bakufu* has cited our national laws as grounds for withholding its consent. That being the case, if the *bakufu* approves trade on this occasion we do not see how there could be any grounds for refusal when other countries made the same request. For the *bakufu* nonetheless to bow to the wishes of Western countries and grant permission for trade would be to take the first step towards destruction of our national strength; it would lead eventually to a policy of humbling ourselves before the might of the foreigners and so impair our national prestige. Moreover, what the foreigners describe as their desire to purchase supplies of coal, food, and so on is but, by another name, the exchange of commodities. It is a trick by which they hope to open trade and is therefore equally inadmissible. Again, mere friendship being a thing that brings no profit, it certainly seems unlikely that the foreigners would press their demands for that alone. Yet it may be that they have some long-range plan in mind which might lead them, on the grounds of proximity of our two countries, to press for an agreement that embodies no more than this. But we have no present need for concluding new friendship agreements with neighboring countries, more particularly as to do so would be in conflict with our national prohibition [against foreign intercourse]. That it is inadmissible is beyond dispute.

Thus, as we have seen, it is impossible for the *bakufu* to accept any single one of the American requests. However, if we return a blunt refusal this will surely displease and disappoint them. It may make them present all manner of demands and even undertake acts of violence. It would be best for the *bakufu* simply to explain that it must adhere to the national laws, but saying so in such a friendly manner as will not make us seem to be acting in bad faith, behaving generally in such a way as to convince them that in present circumstances they have no option but to sail home. However, these foreigners have claimed to be different from those who came before and have said that when they come again next spring they will bring several great warships with them. Moreover when they arrived a short time ago, and the *bakufu* knowing that its military preparations were inadequate, acted peacefully and agreed to accept their letters, they even went so far as to enter Edo Bay and carry out surveys here and there. It does not seem likely, therefore, that they will make no difficulty, that they will return home empty-handed after a mere routine explanation from us. Indeed we are greatly concerned that, despising us, they may continue to press their demands. All foreign countries have been covertly eyeing our land for many years. And though one may belittle the importance of the proposal concerning "an important matter" made by the Dutch king some years ago, if one considers it closely one sees that it was no mere passing whim. More particularly, if one studies the letter in which the new Dutch Kapitan at Nagasaki, acting on the orders of the Governor-General in Batavia, last year forwarded a report from his king on this matter, one finds that it differs only in detail from the demands now brought by the American ships and omits none of the stipulations. Putting these facts together it seems clear that there is a connection. Next year is that in which the Dutch Kapitan is to have his regular audience with the Shōgun. We very much suspect, therefore, that in fact both [Dutch and Americans] are in collusion in a cunning plot to betray us, that they will proceed in accordance with an agreed plan that they have prepared in advance, by which the American ships will time the date of their return next spring to coincide with the coming of the new Dutch Kapitan to Edo: if the nature of our negotiating makes it desirable they will then take military action and so throw the capital into confusion, whereupon the Kapitan, making use of the opportunity and of the fact that he is supposedly experienced in the ways of foreign countries, will intervene to settle the dispute and so ensure that the foreigners succeed in gaining their ends. Might not this be so? At all events, it will be impossible to handle matters effectively unless the *bakufu* now acts so as to intensify defense preparations and devise means by which we may obtain victory even if the foreigners adopt illegal and violent methods, should matters reach a major crisis in which peace and war are brought to issue.

We understand that the foreigners surveyed various places in Edo Bay when they sailed through there recently, even the straits between Awa and Sagami provinces which we regard as the most important of all strategic areas. Should it happen that they conceive ill-will towards us and sail at once to the capital, bombarding it with heavy guns and destroying the city's dwellings by fire, there would be great confusion in the city and it would naturally be impossible for the feudal lords to carry out defense measures. Again, should they, in order to get control of the straits at Urage, seize the Ize Islands and establish a base there, equipping it with guns and ships of every size, they could interrupt our coastal shipping and exhaust the rice and other commodities in Edo. The situation would then, indeed, be most critical, and we are therefore anxious now that the *bakufu* should decide what practical steps to take by sending men now to inspect the coastal areas and report their ideas on the subject after seeing the actual places; and that it should act with all speed, for the time being setting all else aside.

Nonetheless, however much the *bakufu* exerts itself to strengthen our land defenses, the foreigners will be able to anchor wherever they choose and will come and go freely in our coastal waters. Each time they do so the defending forces, from the *daimyō* down, will exhaust themselves in ceaseless activity; and it is possible that this may bring about national collapse, arousing the people's resentment at last [against the *bakufu*] and giving rise to some unlooked-for disaster in domestic affairs. Thus it will be impossible to regard the *bakufu*'s preparations as adequate or complete unless it builds powerful warships and gives orders for training in their use, thus setting up sea-borne defenses to meet and overcome the foreign ships at sea when they come. It is therefore our hope that the *bakufu* will now issue immediate orders that all those responsible for land defense are to undertake also the construction of warships and that both land and sea training is to be carried out, thus ensuring that morale is raised and military preparations completed. Once this is done our strength will be ample to meet whatever violence the foreigners may use and the *bakufu* can negotiate a settlement without fear of difficulties arising.

No matter how earnestly the *bakufu* exerts itself to complete these military preparations, however, it is doubtful whether success can be achieved in the space of one or two years. In the meanwhile, and as a temporary expedient, it would be wise for the *bakufu* to plan its actions in such a manner that hostilities do not break out. Accordingly, having given full and careful thought to the reply the *bakufu* should make, we believe it essential in present circumstances that our action provide the foreigners with no pretext for raising objections, and hence consider the most suitable reply to be as follows:

> It is not unreasonable of America to have sought trade and friendship with us on the grounds that our two countries are neighbors, and in some circumstance we would be willing to agree as long as this were restricted to America. However . . . it is the ancient rule of our country that trade is limited to the Dutch and Chinese. Already, before this, various Western Countries have requested trade, and each time we have

> refused on the grounds that our national laws prohibit it. Yet if these countries learn that we have now permitted America to trade, they will certainly make this a pretext for renewing their requests. In that event we would have no grounds for refusal. Not only that, but also, of course, there is the fact that we have no products that we can exchange. This must be clearly understood. As to coal, our land is very fertile, but our population equally is large and there is no surplus to meet foreign requirements.
>
> On such occasions as ships have suffered damage in our waters, as long as it was beyond doubt that this was a case of shipwreck, we have shown the crews every kindness, have taken action to ensure the safety of their goods, and have sent them back to their own country in Dutch ships. Such having been our action on previous occasions, it must be clearly understood that there is no need to raise this matter. And apart from the question of kind treatment for castaways, the other requests are all matters which it is impossible to arrange. You must therefore understand that, conditions being what they are in Japan, you can do no other than depart at once, never to return again hereafter.

It might happen, however, that the foreigners will not accept this answer and become vehement on the subject. If so, it would not be possible for the *bakufu* to have peace and yet insist on refusing the things which they so earnestly request. We think it would then be best to inform them that it might be possible in certain circumstances for the *bakufu* to permit trade if it were strictly confined to the Americans, but that it is difficult for us to tell exactly whether other Western countries would then seek trade with us; that we therefore want the Americans to conduct discussions with the other countries and, if there are no objections from them to our permitting trade only with America, to notify the Dutch of that fact so that we may be informed through Nagasaki; and that we would then be willing to discuss the agreement they have just proposed. If we were to do this, they would have no pretext for further discussion. The negotiations would thus be made to last for some years; and while they were going on the *bakufu* should take action to complete its preparations both by land and sea. What we have proposed above, about America conducting negotiations with other Western countries and carrying on discussions to ensure that there will be no demands for trade from those other countries, is something they would find quite impossible to accomplish. In effect, therefore, it is a method by which the *bakufu* may postpone the question for the time being. However, since there is no telling what kind of tricks they may use to deceive us simply for the sake of opening trade, the *bakufu* should first give instructions to the Dutch that they are to inform us when these discussions have been completed. If we should be informed [by the Americans] through Holland that all the negotiations in this matter have been completed, we may then inquire more fully of the Dutch. Once they have told us that this is fact and not error we may, on the basis of this report, permit the Americans to trade, though setting a limit of a specific term of years to the agreement. If the other foreigners then renew their demands, we can make that a pretext for immediately banning trade. Alternatively, it may be possible to ban it on the grounds that the *bakufu*, on consideration, finds that trade brings no advantage. Whatever we do we will be buying a stratagem to last till the *bakufu* can complete its military preparations. Hence even if the *bakufu* agrees to permit trade for a time, this will only be a policy devised as a temporary expedient for the purpose of continuing the tradition [of seclusion] that we have maintained for so many generations; and we therefore think that such action can be taken without self-reproach.

Document 19

"Proposal for Reforming Japan, 1862" by Yokoi Shōnan[21]

In the years between Commodore Perry's first visit in 1853 and the Meiji Restoration in 1868, Yokoi Shōnan (1809–1869) became an influential councilor to the Tokugawa government. His proposals for reforming the Tokugawa system were grounded in Confucian ideology (see below the references to the empire of Yao and Shun, the Yui kung, the Nine Classics, etc.) but were nonetheless progressive for the era. He attributed many of the problems in Japan to daimyō *ownership of domains, a system that emphasized the needs of small fiefdoms over the nation as a whole. He believed that this system, combined with misrule, willful neglect, and the exploitation of the common people, placed Japan in its weak position. His willingness to criticize the Tokugawa administration placed him at odds with conservative elements within Japan and he was assassinated. Nonetheless, his assessment of Japan's weaknesses now seems to have been largely correct and many of his suggestions for how best to reform the country were eventually adopted by the Meiji leadership.*

If the basic principles in governing the nation are to be abandoned and only trade and intercourse are to hold sway, should we consider all Western ways as being desirable and make them the practice of the land?

Because of the fact that in recent years trade has been proposed by foreign countries, the average person believes that this was the start of commercial intercourse, but this is by no means the truth. From the very beginning commerce with foreign countries has been an important part of the trade of a country, and its path has been firmly fixed by principles of heaven and earth. Those who rule others must be nourished by the latter, and those who nourish must be ruled. This is the way of trade, and the same applies to government. Nourishing the people is the main work. The administration of the Six Offices and the Three Ministries is no different from trade. In the Six Offices of Water, Fire, Metal, Wood, Earth,

21. Yokoi Shōnan, "Proposal for Reforming Japan, 1862." Found in Dixon Y. Miyauchi, ed. and trans., "Kokuze Sanron. The Three Major Problems of State Policy," *Monumenta Nipponica* 23, no 1–2 (1968): 166–170.

and Cereal the strength of soil and of men are added to mountains, rivers, and the seas. The activities of the people are benefited, and their living is made more harmonious. This is the principle of Nature (*shizen no jōri*). The rule of the empire of Yao and Shun was none other than this.

The work of trade involves the cutting of the nine rivers and having them flow into all the seas, the deepening of ditches, and the spanning of rivers in order to supply the deficiencies of a place, thereby making it habitable; in other words, to open up waterways for the passage of ships so that the people can be fed. The "Yui kung" in particular records that according to the nature of the land, products such as gold, silver, lead, iron, mulberry, and dyed fibers should be developed; rivers, seas, mountains, and swamps should be utilized in a beneficial way; and a tax system should be set up. In this way the administration of large-scale trade would of course make an outstanding record. The Eight Ministries should give priority to the problem of food and money, the common people should be made pupils of the Nine Classics; and many artisans should be developed. All these constitute the good teachings and the benevolent governments which have been established by the great sages, and they make up the books of the great classics which will guide countless generations.

In our country from the middle ages wars have followed in succession, the Imperial Court has become weak, and various lords have parceled out groups of provinces, each defending his own territory while attacking others in turn. The people were looked upon as so much waste, and the severity of forced labor and the arbitrary collection of military rations knew no bounds. Good government was swept away from the land, and it was a period in which one who was skilled in warfare became a great lord and one who was clever in planning became a renowned minister.

Consequently in the Keicho (1596–1615) and Genna (1615–1624) periods, when a period of peace had come, these old ways remained. The great retainers on the war council, including Honda Sado-no-kami (1538–1616), all strove to make the foundation of the Tokugawa household supreme and firm, and not once was consideration given to the people of the realm. Although there are said to have been many outstanding rulers and ministers from that time to the present, all have continued the work of administering the private affairs of one household only. The various lords have followed this pattern, and according to the old ways handed down from their ancestors, they have planned with their ministers for the convenience and security of their own provinces with a barrier between neighboring provinces.

As a result those who are known as great ministers in the shōgunate and in each of the provinces have not all been able to disentangle themselves from the old ways of national seclusion. They have devoted themselves to their lords and their provinces, while their feelings of love and loyalty for the most part ignore the virtues of the good life and on the contrary invite the resentment of the people. All this leads to troubles in ruling the land. Japan has been split up thusly and lacks a unified system. Therefore we must admit that Envoy Perry's observation in his *Expedition to Japan* about the lack of government machinery in Japan when he arrived here in 1855 was truly a discerning one.

Although forbidden, let us discuss the detested things of the present day. From the very beginning the shōgunate anticipated moves by the various lords, and the system it used to weaken their military potential was to impose on them the *sankin kotai* practice, the construction of large and small projects, the fire watches on the two sacred mountain precincts, and guard duty at the highway barrier stations. Moreover, in recent years the guarding of the countryside has been extremely burdensome, yet no consideration has been given to the drain on the provinces and their people. Furthermore, all systems, including currency, are transmitted and executed throughout the land by the power of the supreme government in the interest of the Tokugawa household without in any way benefiting the empire or the people. For Perry to call this "lack of government" was indeed correct.

Under the system of national seclusion Japan sought safety in isolation. Hence she experienced no wars or defeats. However, the world situation has undergone vast changes. Each country has broadly developed enlightened government.

In America three major policies have been set up from Washington's presidency on: First, to stop wars in accordance with divine intentions, because nothing is worse than violence and killing among nations; second, to broaden enlightened government by learning from all the countries of the world; and third, to work with complete devotion for the peace and welfare of the people by entrusting the power of the president of the whole country to the wisest instead of transmitting it to the son of the president and by abolishing the code in the relationship between ruler and minister. All methods of administrative laws and practices and all men who are known as good and wise throughout the world are put into the country's service and a very beneficial administration, one not completely in the interest of the rulers, is developed.

In England the government is based entirely on the popular will, and all government actions, large and small, are always debated by the people. The most beneficial action is decided upon, and an unpopular program is not forced upon the people. War or peace is decided thusly. When there were wars lasting several years against Russia and against China at a huge cost in men and money, all taken from the people, not one person complained against them. Furthermore, all countries, including Russia, have established schools and military academies, hospitals, orphanages, and schools for the deaf and dumb. The governments are entirely based on moral principles, and they work hard for the benefit of the people, virtually as in the three ancient periods of sage-rule in China.

Thus when the various countries attempt to open Japan's doors according to the way of international cooperation, who would not call Japan a fool for persisting in her old seclusionist views, for ruling for the benefit of private interests, and for not knowing the principles of commercial intercourse?

Document 20

The United States Seeks Special Access to Some of Japan's Harbors (1855)[22]

The United States Navy sent a squadron to survey the North Pacific between 1853 and 1856. After the first commander, Cadwalader Ringgold, was removed from duty, John Rodgers assumed command. Rodgers sought special permission from the Japanese government to enter Japanese territorial waters and to sometimes land to check the accuracy of charts and recalibrate instruments. From the tone of the correspondence below, it is clear that Commander Rodgers did not completely understand the scope of the agreement signed the year before with Commodore Perry. His reference to the possible use of force echoes Commodore Perry's attitude of the previous years and can best be described as condescending and impolitic. His request, which was denied, appears to have perplexed the Japanese who were in no mood to allow the United States additional concessions. Indeed, the Japanese letter indicates that there could be "unpleasant difficulties"—coded language for possible hostilities. This was a tense situation and is one of the interactions between Japan and the United States that motivated the signing of the Harris Treaty in 1858.

To the Honorable Secretary of State
for Foreign Affairs
Kingdom of Japan

U.S. Ship *Vincennes*
Kago Sima Bay
January 4, 1855

Sir!

This Government of the United States sent five vessels, of which this is the chief, to examine the dangers of the Ocean. We have been round more than half the Globe. We have at last arrived at one of the Japanese ports. If the Islands of Japan with the rocks and shoals which surround them, were out of the paths which our vessels follow across the Ocean, the world could say nothing, but as these dangers remain in the road of ships, we

22. Found in Allen B. Cole, ed., *Yankee Surveyors in the Shogun's Seas: Records of the United States Surveying Expedition to the North Pacific 1853–1856* (Princeton, NJ: Princeton University Press, 1947), pp. 48–49.

must examine them, and tell our countrymen where they lie. Otherwise our vessels would be wrecked, and many valuable lives might be lost.

We find our way across seas by certain instruments and observations of heavenly bodies. But as some of the instruments, called chronometers, are liable to go wrong, it is absolutely necessary to make examinations from time to time, of whether they perform well, and to correct their rates.

It happens, that the astronomical observations for the error of these instruments must be made on the land, because a vessel is too unsteady for very delicate observations.

Why need friends hesitate to speak plainly? From want of clearness and of mutual understanding, difficulties arise. We must go on shore to take astronomical observations.

We are in distress without them!

I am sure the Government of Japan, and my own Government, would not thank any Japanese officer who should compel me to use force in taking necessary astronomical observations.

I say this because in a few months my own vessel, or one or more of those under my command, will, in the prosecution of our duties, probably stop at some port in Japan, and I earnestly hope no too ardent officer will by his overzeal bring himself and me into trouble.

I have the honour to be your respectful friend,

(Signed) John Rodgers, U.S.N.
Commanding U.S. Surveying Expedition to
the North Pacific Ocean &c

The Response from Japan[23]

His Excellency Commander John Rodgers

My Sir

It has been said that some of your squadron on their voyage North want to sail in a boat along the coast of our Empire, and that if wanting water run into the nearest harbor. On the grounds of the treaty with the U.S. our nation is of the opinion that the ships of the U.S. are allowed

23. "Correspondence between Lord Izawa Mimasaki-no-kami and Commander John Rodgers." Found in Cole, ed., *Yankee Surveyors in the Shogun's Seas*, p. 66.

no other harbors than those of Simoda and Hakodidi, except in storm or distress. Should a vessel want only run into any harbor it cannot be sure that there may not occur unpleasant difficulties, and our friendship might be really weakened. So it is impossible to concur in your wish to run into other harbors as long as there is not given a favorable, or unfavorable answer, to your written application, which shortly ago was handed to the Government.

The 10th of the 4th Month 1855

(Signed) Izawa Mimasakanokami
[Izawa Mimasaka-no-kami]

(Signed) Tsoedzoeki Soerroeganokami
[Suzuki Sūrūga-no-kami]

(Signed) Inowoeje Sinjemon
[Inouye Sinyemon]

Document 21

Journal Entry of Townsend Harris, First U.S. Envoy to Japan, Tuesday August 27, 1856[24]

The Japanese government was surprised when Townsend Harris arrived in Japan to take up residence as consul general. From the passage below, it is clear that the Japanese government had made no preparations for his arrival and, indeed, was not expecting a U.S. envoy at all. Nonetheless, Harris went ashore on August 23 and began his official duties. In Harris's description, one can sense just how awkward these initial meetings were for him and the Japanese government. Nonetheless, in 1858, Harris successfully negotiated a more comprehensive treaty between the United States and Japan.

I omitted yesterday to state that a superior interpreter appeared at my interview. He is attached to the office of the Minister for Foreign Affairs; a good interpreter, of most agreeable manners and a true courtier. Seven scribes recorded our sayings and doings yesterday. Today ashore at ten with Mr. Heuksen. Met with Vice-Governor and the person from Yedo [Edo/Tokyo], who evidently has come down since our arrival was reported there, although they say the journey cannot be made under five days from here to Yedo. My interview was long and far from satisfactory. To sum it is all I shall attempt. They did not expect the arrival of a Consul, a Consul was only to be sent when some difficulty arose, and no such thing had taken place. That Shimoda was a poor place and had been recently desolated by an earthquake; that they had no residence prepared for me; that I had better go away and return in about a year, when they hoped to have a house ready. The treaty said that a Consul was to come if both nations wished it; that it was not left to the simple will of the United States Government.

Would I land at Kakizaki, and take up my residence at the temple there, and leave the question of my official residence to be settled by

24. "Tuesday August 26, 1856." Found in William Elliot Griffis, *Townsend Harris: First American Envoy in Japan* (London: Sampson Low, Marston & Company, 1895), pp. 42–43.

future negotiations? Yedo was also in a ruinous condition from the earthquake ten months since, therefore they could not offer me a house there while building one here.

The foregoing is the substance of their remarks and propositions, made and renewed and changed in every possible form and manner during three mortal hours. I need hardly write that I courteously but firmly negated all their propositions. They earnestly protested against the idea that they refused to receive me, or that they meant in any way to break the Treaty. They at least begged to adjourn the business until tomorrow at the same hour, to give them time to consult. The sales in the bazaar cannot be much under two thousand dollars. The prices are most exorbitant. They appear to raise them at each new arrival of a ship here. Ordered spars to make flagstaff; one of fifty feet, twelve inches by eight, and the other thirty feet long, seven inches by four inches, and four small pieces.

Document 22

Convention between Great Britain and Japan (1854)[25]

Many of Japan's leaders were concerned that the treaty signed with the United States in 1854 would be only the first of many forced on the Japanese by the Western powers. These fears were well founded. Within six months, the British appeared and demanded a treaty. However, the geopolitical situation had changed since Commodore Perry's first visit. News of the Crimean War (1853–1856) had reached East Asia and the British were actively hunting Russian vessels. Accordingly, British Vice Admiral James Stirling sailed into Nagasaki harbor after hearing that the Russians had recently visited. Finding no Russian vessels, Stirling sought assurances of Japanese neutrality and asked the Japanese to not allow the Russians to use any of its ports. The Japanese, on the other hand, wondered whether Britain could act as a counterweight to the Russians in the northern territories. Stirling was not empowered by the admiralty to sign a treaty with the Japanese. But when it was offered, he wasted no time signing it.

Signed at Nagasaki, October 14th 1854.
Ratified by Her Britannic Majesty, January 23rd, 1855.
Ratifications exchanged at Nagasaki, October 9th, 1855.

It is agreed between Sir James Stirling, Knight, Rear-Admiral and Commander-in-chief of the ships and vessels of Her Britannic Majesty in the East Indies and seas adjacent, and Mezi-no Chekfu-no Kami, Obunyo of Nagasaki, and Nagai Evan Ocho, Omedski of Nagasaki, ordered by His Imperial Highness the Emperor of Japan to act herein; that

25. "Treaties and Conventions Concluded Between Japan and Foreign Nations, Together with Notifications & Regulations Made from Time to Time," *Daily Japan Herald* (Yokohama), 1871, pp. 6–7.

I.

The ports of Nagasaki (Fisen) and Hakodadi (Matsmai) shall be open to British ships for the purposes of effecting repairs, and obtaining fresh water, provisions, and other supplies of any sort they may absolutely want for the use of the ships.

II.

Nagasaki shall be open for the purposes aforesaid from and after the present date; and Hakodadi from and after the end of fifty days from the Admiral's departure from this port. The rules and regulations of each of these ports are to be complied with.

III.

Only ships in distress from weather or unmanageable will be permitted to enter other ports than those specified in the foregoing Articles, without permission from the Imperial Government.

IV.

British ships in Japanese ports shall conform to the laws of Japan. If high officers or commanders of ships shall break any such laws, it will lead to the ports being closed. Should inferior persons break them, they are to be delivered over to the Commanders of their ships for punishment.

V.

In the ports of Japan either now open, or which may hereafter be opened, to the ships or subjects of any foreign nation, British ships and subjects shall be entitled to admission and to the enjoyment of an equality of advantages with those of the most favoured nation, always excepting the advantages accruing to the Dutch and Chinese from their existing relations with Japan.

VI.

This Convention shall be ratified, and the ratifications shall be exchanged at Nagasaki on behalf of Her Majesty the Queen of Great Britain, and on behalf of His Highness the Emperor of Japan, within twelve months from the present date.

VII.

When this Convention shall be ratified, no high officer coming to Japan shall alter it.

In witness whereof we have signed the same, and have affixed our seals thereunto, at Nagasaki, this fourteenth day of October, 1854.

(L. S.) JS. STIRLING

Document 23

Treaty between Russia and Japan (1855)[26]

The treaty below was signed in the midst of the Crimean War (1853–1856) between Russia and Great Britain. The hostilities between two of the world's largest empires caused the Japanese no small amount of consternation. Less than eleven months after Japan's reengagement with the world via their first treaty with the United States, they had also signed a treaty with the British . . . and now the Russians were making similar ultimatums. The series of demands made one after the other by powerful Western imperialists confirmed one of Japan's greatest fears. Nonetheless, the Japanese believed they had no choice other than to sign. The treaty below is the result of many months of negotiations between Admiral Yevfirm Putyatin and Tsutsui Hizen and Kawaji Saemon no jō. It is not surprising that there are many similarities among the U.S., British, and Russian treaties.

Signed at Shimoda, February 7th, 1855

The countries of Russia and Japan being at peace and desiring to preserve friendly relations, and having the intention of concluding a Treaty, the Czar of Russia has named as his Plenipotentiary, Adjutant General, Vice-Admiral Poutiatine, and the Tycoon of Japan has named his ministers Tsutsui Hizen no Kami and Kawaji Sayemon no Jo, who have agreed upon the following Articles:

I.

The two powers from this time forth being on terms of true friendship shall mutually in their respective countries protect the lives and property of one another's subjects, so that they shall suffer neither loss nor injury.

26. "Treaties and Conventions Concluded Between Japan and Foreign Nations, Together with Notifications & Regulations Made from Time to Time," pp. 8–9.

II.

From henceforth the boundary of Japan and Russia shall be between the islands of Yetorofu (Iturup) and Urutsufu (Urup). The island of Iturup belongs entirely to Japan; the whole island of Urup together with the several Kurile islands to the north thereof are the possessions of Russia. As for the island of Karafuto (Saghalin), which is between the possessions of Russia and those of Japan, no boundary line is drawn; it shall remain as it had hitherto been.

III.

The Government of Japan agrees to open to Russian shipping the three ports of Hakodate, Shimoda, and Nagasaki. From henceforth Russian ships may repair damages and may lay in wood, water, and such stores as they may be in want of, and, further, in places where coal is to be had, it shall be supplied to them. Payment shall be made in gold, silver, or copper cash, and if the Russian ships have no such money they may pay in goods. Except in cases of distress Russian ships may not put into any Japanese harbor other than the three specified above; and any expenses incurred on account of such distress shall be paid at one of the three above ports.

IV.

Shipwrecked persons driven on shore shall be well cared for by the contracting Powers and sent to one of the open ports. They will be treated kindly and with leniency, but they must abide by the laws of the country.

V.

Russian ships arriving at Shimoda or Hakodate, may purchase such articles as they may stand in need of, paying for the same in gold, silver, or in merchandize.

VI.

In case of necessity the Russian Government may appoint an officer to reside at Hakodate or Shimoda.

VII.

Should any question arise involving a delay for further deliberation, the Japanese Government undertakes (in the meanwhile) to direct the matter with the utmost consideration.

VIII.

Russian subjects living in Japan, and Japanese subjects living in Russia will be treated kindly and with leniency, and will be subjected to no restrictions of liberty; should they offend against the laws, however, they will be arrested and punished according to the laws of their own country.

IX.

The two countries being near neighbors, should Japan after the conclusion of this treaty, grant any privileges to other countries, the same privileges will at the same time be extended to Russian subjects.

The above Treaty will be ratified, in a separate form, by the Czar of Russia and the Tycoon of Japan, and the ratifications will be exchanged at Shimoda, at a convenient time, after a lapse of nine months.

In token of which the Plenipotentiaries of the two countries have affixed their respective signatures and seals.

The stipulations of the Treaty shall be observed without variations or alterations.

First Year of Ansei, 12th month, 21st day.

(February 7th, 1855)
(Signed) Tsutsui Hizen no Kami
(Signed) Kawaji Sayemon no Jo

Document 24

Murder in Yokohama (1859)[27]

In the years immediately after the signing of the second round of treaties with the Western powers, there was an increasing sense of unease and foreboding in Japan. Several domains, such as Chōshū and Mito, began to openly question the decisions of the Tokugawa. Others fired on foreign ships against the explicit orders of the Tokugawa and paid the price for their actions by being bombarded and chastised by those same foreigners. On land, a movement was afoot to destabilize the government, and foreigners were attacked and assassinated by rogue samurai. Below is an example of an attempted attack on a foreigner. In this 1859 episode in Yokohama, a Japanese servant wearing the cloak of his foreign employer was cut down on a dark, rainy night in a case of mistaken identity. The Japanese representative tasked with addressing the issue among various groups of foreigners found himself in very delicate negotiations. There were multiple, aggrieved parties, all from different countries. It was a precarious diplomatic situation. This passage also reveals, surprisingly, the weak position the Westerners occupied in Japan. In the end, all parties seemed to have been satisfied. There is no record of what reparations were provided to the family of the deceased.

The next day at the Interpreters' office I complained to the interpreter Sakfsabro about the hellish racket that the night watch had made, and the terror that had resulted.

"I am very sorry about that," said my friend, "but I shall tell you how it came to pass. You know that the night before last one of Loureiro's servants was murdered. Now this gentleman is an agent of an English house as well as a French consular agent, and his servant had just returned from an errand to an English ship. That is why the English and French ministers are making this murder an English and French affair. They along with their secretaries, already came here, to the Interpreters' Office, from

27. "Murder and Extraterritoriality in Yokohama." Found in C. T. Assendelft de Coningh, *A Pioneer in Yokohama*, ed. and trans. Martha Chaiklin (Indianapolis: Hackett Publishing, 2012), pp. 57–59.

Jeddo early yesterday morning and demanded to speak to the Governor. Given that the murder victim was in the service of the English house and had just finished an errand to an English ship, the English minister considered the case of such a serious nature that if hefty reparations were not paid immediately, the English fleet from China would appear in Yokohama. And since Mr. Loureiro was a French consular agent, the French minister considered this affair an affront to French honor, so if French demands were not met, then the French General de Montauban, now in China with his army, knew very well what to do in concert with the English admiral to lead the Japanese government to her duty. After these threats they left with their secretaries, to return in twenty-four hours to hear the answer. The Governor, who had never before had to deal with European politics was, after this parlay, more than a little nervous and agitated; for if the affair was not settled, nothing was left for him but to cut his belly.

"Yesterday morning at ten-thirty, the *dwarskijker* reported to the Interpreters' Office that at ten past ten he had settled you into Josaimon's hut. When we returned yesterday afternoon from our visit to you, we were immediately called to the Governor's office; another *dwarskijker* had already reported that he had seen us go visit you and return. The Governor was still suffering the effects of his interview with the foreign Minister, so when we responded to his question as to whether or not we had made you promise to return to shipboard for the night in the negative, he gave us a thorough reprimand. He hauled us over the coals. Indeed, he thought it would be impossible for a foreigner to make it through the night on the lonesome beach at Josaimon's, and that tomorrow the Dutch Consul would come for his head, asking for reparations and, backed up by the English and French Ministers, threaten war with Holland too.

"We could not argue with this. Meanwhile, the Governor went and called a *banjoost* of the police and ordered three watchmen, with iron rattling staffs like those used at fires in Jeddo, to watch over your house. Their orders were to awaken you with a great racket at least once to personally ascertain that you remained alive and unharmed. By doing so, no mishap could befall you; and if a declaration of war was made, you would be called as a witness to confirm the truth on behalf of the Interpreters' Office, that the lives of foreigners were protected at night."

I thanked Sakfsabro for his explanation, by which I was completely satisfied. "But," I asked him, "tell me something. The twenty-four hours have elapsed. What settlement have the English and French Ministers received, or has the Governor cut his stomach open?"

"Everything has just now been fortuitously resolved," said Sakfsabro, "for the Governor deliberated over the answer with his council last night and one of them is very smart. He's a, how do you call it in Dutch, a—a—twist talker."

"A twist talker?" I asked, puzzled.

"Yes, how do you call that again? Some who is very skillful at twisting affairs with words."

"Maybe you mean a lawyer?" I said.

"Right, exactly, a lawyer. Now, he spoke for the Governor this morning at a meeting about this case. Mr. Loureiro's presence was sought to recount the details of the affair. He related how he had sent his servant on an errand to an English ship and, because it was raining, the servant threw on an old coat. He went on to tell how because of the coat and everything else, assassins had chopped off the servant's head and left shoulder.

"'What was the name of your servant?' asked the lawyer.

"'Tjing-Tjang-la.'

"'Where was he born, in England or France?'

"'In neither, in China.'

"'We don't have a treaty with China,' said the lawyer, 'and your servant was a Chinese. A murdered Chinese doesn't concern us. Thus we will only pay reparations for your coat.'

"'What is your name, if you please?' continued the lawyer.

"'José Loureiro.'

"'Where were you born, in England or France?"

"'In neither, in Portugal.'

"'We have no treaty with Portugal,' said our lawyer, 'and you are a Portuguese. Therefore the Governor must rule that Japan, according to the treaty, has no obligation to pay reparations to France and England for the dead Chinese and a Portuguese coat.'

"On these grounds the business is not resolved, and a great war avoided,'" concluded Sakfsabro.

I was amazed at the wisdom of the Japanese Solomon. But I could have further reassured Sakfsabro that even without the lawyer, the foreign ministers' bluff would have failed. Just at the moment, and for several months thereafter, England and France had their hands so full in China that all the foreigners, down to the last man, were put in arms and for the time being not a single "blue jacket" or "*troupier Francais*" could have been spared to avenge us.

Though I knew this, I was wise enough not to tell any Japanese. Haughty England was so powerless in Japan in those days that for eight months long nothing could be spared for the protection of Englishmen but the *Camilla,* an old sailing brig of 12 guns. In the years of 1859 and 1860 I saw English blush at their weakness compared to other foreigners in Japan, and a blushing Englishman is as rare as a white raven. As for France: in the first frightening months in Yokohama I never saw a single French warship there; all their available expeditionary troops were headed to Peiho under General de Montauban for the mission to Peking.

Document 25

Manifesto Announcing the Shogun's Abdication, November 8, 1867[28]

The last shogun of Japan was Tokugawa Yoshinobu (1837–1913). He was in office only a brief period, from August 1866 to November 1867. Historians depict him as a capable man, but argue that he had little time to institute the reforms needed to stabilize the country. In his notice of abdication, he stated clearly that he wished to see power revert to the emperor. According to the terms of his abdication, he was to chair a new, national governing council imbued with extraordinary authority and tasked with saving the country. But he and his advisors underestimated the extent of the opposition he faced, and he later changed his mind and tried to re-exert power as shogun. This crisis set in motion the events that led to the Meiji Restoration.

Looking at the various changes through which the Empire has passed, we see that when the monarchical authority became weakened, the power was seized by the Ministers of State, and that afterwards, owing to the civil wars of the periods Hōgen (1156–1159) and Heiji (1159–1160), it passed into the hands of the military class. Later on again my ancestor received special favour from the throne (being appointed Shōgun), and his descendants have succeeded him for over 200 years. Though I fill the same office, the laws are often improperly administered, and I confess with shame that the condition of affairs today shows my incapacity. Now that foreign intercourse becomes daily more extensive, unless the Government is directed from one central point, the basis of administration will fall to pieces. If, therefore, the old order of things changed, and the administrative authority be restored to the Imperial Court, if national deliberations be conducted on an extensive scale, and the Imperial decision then invited, and if the Empire be protected with united hearts and combined effort, our country will hold its own with all nations of the world. This is our one duty to our country, but if any persons have other views on the subject they should be stated without reserve.

28. "The Letter of Resignation of the Shogun." Found in Gubbins, *The Progress of Japan, 1853–1871*, p. 305.

Document 26

Charter Oath of April 6, 1868[29]

The Charter Oath is understood by historians to be the founding document of Meiji Japan. Even though the Boshin War (1868–1869), which ushered in the Meiji Restoration, was still raging, the Oath was the first clear statement from Japan's new leaders of their basic goals for the country. Despite its brevity, it makes clear that there was to be a clean break with Japan's feudal past. In particular, the document indicates a desire to institute some democratic reforms, to break down old social structures, to open the country to learning, and to abandon many other Tokugawa practices.

By this oath, we set up as our aim the establishment of the national wealth on a broad basis and the framing of a constitution and laws.

1) Deliberative assemblies shall be widely established and all matters decided by open discussion.

2) All classes, high and low, shall be united in vigorously carrying out the administration of affairs of state.

3) The common people, no less than the civil and military officials, shall all be allowed to pursue their own calling so that there may be no discontent.

4) Evil customs of the past shall be broken off and everything based upon the just laws of Nature.

5) Knowledge shall be sought throughout the world so as to strengthen the foundation of imperial rule.

---

29. Found in W. W. McLaren, *Japanese Government Documents* (Tokyo: Asiatic Society of Japan, 1914), p. 8.

Document 27

The Abolition of Feudalism (1869)[30]

In the months following the Meiji Restoration, the new leadership cast about for ways to reform the country. One of the greatest problems they faced was the lack of a strong central government. In the passage below, the leaders of four key domains demand that feudal authority give way to a central authority led by the emperor. They use the language of "imperial restoration" and appeal to history to support their primary argument. These four clans—the Shimazu of Satsuma, the Mori of Chōshū, the Nabeshima of Saga, and the Yamanouchi of Tosa—were some of the primary supporters of the Meiji Restoration. Therefore, this proposal carried a great deal of moral and implicit authority. A few months after the publication of this proposal, all daimyō *who had not voluntarily turned administration of their domains over to the new central government slowly lost control of their domains. This effectively ended the decentralized political system that characterized the Tokugawa shogunate and created a central government. This was the first major step in the process of consolidating political power in the hands of the Meiji oligarchy.*

The Proposal to Return the Registers

Four western lords, Shimadzu, Mori, Nabeshima, and Yamanouchi propose to give up their fiefs.

March 5, 1869.

Text of the Proposal

Your servants again venture to address Your Majesty with profound reverence. Two things are essential to the Mikado's[31] administration. There

30. "The Abolition of Feudalism in 1869." Found in McLaren, *Japanese Government Documents*, pp. 29–32.

31. An old name for Japan.

must be one central body of government, and one universal authority which must be preserved intact. Since the time when Your Majesty's ancestors founded this country and established a basis of government, all things in the wide expanse of heaven and all things on earth to its furthest limits, have belonged to the Emperor from generation to generation. This is what is known as "one central government." And the sole power of giving and of taking away, which renders it impossible for the nobles to hold the people in subjection in virtue of their land, or to deal with the smallest piece of ground at their pleasure, or to seize and treat despotically any individual of the humbler classes, this is what is understood by the term "one universal authority."

The administration of the Emperors was conducted entirely on this principle. They conducted the government in their own persons, the name and reality of power were combined, and consequently the nation was tranquil and contented. But from the time of the middle ages the administration became lax, and the authority of the Emperors came to be a plaything. All men fighting for power, changes of government followed each other in rapid succession, until half of the country fell into the hands of men who dealt with the people and the land at their pleasure; and in the end a state of things was reached where there was nothing but open contention and acts of violence. The government having no body of administration to protect, and no effective power, was unable to control matters. Everywhere men of influence, but of unprincipled character, took advantage of the existing disorder to promote their own interests, and the weak became food for the strong.

The most powerful barons took possession of fourteen or fifteen provinces, while those of less influence collected bodies of armed retainers to the number of five or six thousand. Successive Shōguns seized land and people arbitrarily whenever they thought fit, and by this means extended their influence. Finally the Mikado's government lost all real authority, and was entirely dependent upon the will of the Shōgunate. The boundless despotism of the Shōgunate lasted for over six hundred years, and during this interval violent dealings with land and with the people were carried out by stealth under pretense of the Imperial authority. These acts were rendered possible owing to the existence of people who could not dissociate themselves from the time-honored observances of the past, and were still guided by the reverence due from a subject to his sovereign, and by a proper sense of the relation which should exist between high and low.

The ancient family of the Tokugawa dynasty of Shoguns and their relatives held half the country; as a natural consequence fresh families were constantly springing up; and it became a precedent founded on long custom which has lasted up till the present time for these numerous branches of the Tokugawa family to take no heed of the question as to whether their lands and subjects had been received in grant from the proper Government or not. It was commonly said by members of these families: "These possessions of ours were gained by the military power of our ancestors." But there is little doubt that those ancestors had originally raised forces, plundered the Imperial store-houses, and laid forcible hands on the treasures contained, and had braved the penalty of death in the execution of their designs. Those who break into store-houses are commonly termed robbers, but no suspicion was attached by the nation to those who seized upon the land and people. It is terrible indeed this confusion between right and wrong.

It is now sought to establish an entirely new form of government. Care must, therefore, be taken to preserve intact both one central body of government, and one universal authority. The land in which your servants live is the land of the Emperor, and the people whom they govern are his subjects. Neither the one, therefore, nor the other can belong to your servants.

Your servants accordingly beg respectfully to surrender to Your Majesty the registers of the population, and beg Your Majesty to deal with everything as you may think fit, giving what should be given and taking away what should be taken away. They entreat Your Majesty to issue such Imperial Decrees as may be deemed necessary to deal with the lands and people of the four clans represented in this memorial, and to make such changes as Your Majesty may think proper. They also beg that all laws, decrees, and military regulations, extending even to military dress and accoutrements, may be issued by the Central government, so that all matters of state may be decided by one and the same authority. In this way both name and reality will be secured, and this country will be placed upon a footing of equality with foreign powers.

Your servants share the responsibility which the present critical condition of affairs entails upon the Mikado's government. It is this which has led them to represent their foolish views for the consideration of Your Majesty.

Document 28

Conscription Regulations (1873)[32]

Feudal lords (daimyō) *had been responsible for the administration of their private domains during the entirety of Tokugawa period. Each* daimyō *fed, housed, trained, equipped, and commanded all the samurai in his private military. The* daimyō *then provided samurai as requested by the shogun. After the domains were formally abolished in 1871, there was no military, and the new Meiji governing elites created a conscript army. It was led by Yamagata Aritomo (1838–1922), who had traveled to Europe in 1869 to study French and German (Prussian) models. Yamagata felt an affinity with Prussia, especially after their victory over the French in the Franco-Prussian War (1870–1871) and used that country's military as a model for Japan's.*

From the 1st of January next, conscription is to be enforced in all parts of the country. Five men for every 10,000 *koku* are to be called. No regard is to be paid to the social position of the people; men who are strong and serviceable are to be chosen.

Regulations

I. Those who are chosen must be between twenty and thirty years of age, five feet (shaku) at least in height, strongly built and serviceable. They have however to pass an examination for conscription.

II. The head of a family, or a son who has old or disabled parents dependent upon him, must not be conscripted.

III. Those chosen are to serve four years. To those who have finished their service and are about to return home a sum of money is to be given according to their rank and grade.

During the term of service men are not allowed to return home for any private reason whatsoever. After the completion of their term they may remain longer in the service, if they desire to do so.

IV. Aid is to be given to those who have been disabled for life while on duty during their term of service.

---

32. "Regulations on Conscription." Found in McLaren, *Japanese Government Documents*, pp. 17–18.

V. Food, clothing, and pay are to be supplied to the men called out through the Department of the Army and Navy (Hyōbushō).

Travelling expenses to the place of service (Ōsaka) are to be paid by the locality from which the recruit comes; but to those who have completed the term of service their travelling expenses home will be defrayed by the central government.

VI. If any candidate fails to pass the examination for conscription then a substitute for him must be sent by the locality. In such a case the travelling expenses both coming and returning must be paid by the locality.

VII. All expenses except those above mentioned are to be paid by the central authorities.

VIII. Those selected for conscription by the local authorities are to be sent to the Agency of the Department of the Army and Navy at Ōsaka.

January 3, 1871.

Document 29

Letter from the Emperor of Japan to President Ulysses S. Grant on the Occasion of the Iwakura Embassy's Visit to the United States (1872)[33]

The Iwakura Embassy's world tour began on the West Coast of the United States and the North American leg ended, many months later, in New York and Boston. This "study tour" was perhaps the most important event in the early Meiji years, after the Restoration itself. The letter below serves several functions. It conveys information about the goals of the Iwakura Embassy (1871–1873); presents the names, titles, and bona fides of the ambassadors of the mission; and indicates a desire to improve diplomatic relations with the United States. Of particular note, the emperor seeks to have the unequal treaties revised as soon as possible. (This didn't happen in a comprehensive way until the twentieth century.) In addition, the emperor indicates he is aware of Japan's weaknesses and seeks to remedy them, in part, through learning as much about the Western powers as possible and by adopting the structures of their best institutions. This was a striking admission by the leader of any country, but conveyed the seriousness of their reform efforts.

"Our Good Brother and Faithful Friend, Greeting:

"Mr. President: Whereas, since our accession by the blessing of Heaven to the sacred throne on which our ancestors reigned from time immemorial, we have not dispatched any embassy to the courts and Governments of friendly countries: We have thought fit to select our trusty and honoured Minister Sionii Tomomi Iwakura, the Junior Prime Minister, as Ambassador Extraordinary, and have associated with him Iussammi Takayossi Kido, member of Privy Council; Iussammi Tossimitsi Okubo, Minister of Finance; Iushie Hirobumie Ito, Acting Minister of Public Works; and Iushie Masouha Yamugutsi, Assistant Minister for Foreign Affairs, Associate Ambassadors Extraordinary, and invested them with

33. Letter from "Moutsoukito, Emperor of Japan, &c., to the President of the United States." Found in Charles Lanman, ed., *The Japanese in America* (London: Longmans, Green, Reader, and Dyer, 1872), pp. 36–38.

full powers to proceed to the Government of the United States, as well as to other Governments, in order to declare our cordial friendship, and to place the peaceful relations between our respective nations on a firmer and broader basis.

"The period for revising the treaties now existing between ourselves and the United States is less than one year distant. We expect and intend to reform and improve the same so as to stand upon a similar footing with the most enlightened nations, and to attain the full development of public right and interest. The civilization and institutions of Japan are so different from those of other countries that we cannot expect to reach the desired end at once.

"It is our purpose to select from the various institutions prevailing among enlightened nations such as are best suited to our present condition, and adopt them, in graduate reforms and improvements of our policy and customs, so as to be upon an equality with them.

"With this object, we desire to fully disclose to the United States Government the condition of affairs in our Empire and to consult upon the means of giving greater efficiency to our institutions, at present and in the future; and as soon as the said Embassy returns home we will consider about the revision of the treaties, and accomplish what we have expected and intended.

"The Ministers who compose this Embassy have our confidence and esteem. We request you to favour them with full credence and due regard; and we earnestly pray for your continued health and happiness, and for the peace and prosperity of your great Republic.

"In witness whereof we have hereunto set our hand and the great seal of our Empire, at our palace, in the city of Tokio, this 4th of eleventh month, or the fourth year of Meiji.

"Your affectionate brother and friend,

"Moutsoukito"

BIBLIOGRAPHY

Beasley, W. G. *The Meiji Restoration*. Stanford, CA: Stanford University Press, 1972. Reissued by Lexington Books in 2000.

———. *Select Documents on Japanese Foreign Policy, 1853–1868*. Oxford: Oxford University Press, 1955.

Blodget, H. "A Sketch of the Life and Services of the Late S.W. Williams, LLD." *The Chinese Recorder and Missionary Journal* XV (May–June 1884): 217.

Botsman, Daniel V. *Punishment and Power in the Making of Modern Japan*. Princeton, NJ: Princeton University Press, 2007.

Breen, John. "The Imperial Oath of April 1868: Ritual, Politics, and Power in the Restoration." *Monumenta Nipponica* 51, no. 4 (Winter 1996): 407–429.

Centre for East Asian Cultural Studies. *Meiji Japan through Contemporary Sources*. Vol. 2, *1844–1882*. Tokyo: Toyo Bunko, 1969.

"Commodore Perry's Fleet" as depicted in an 1853 woodblock print. Yokohama City Public Library collection.

Cole, Allan B., ed. *Yankee Surveyors in the Shogun's Seas: Records of the United States Surveying Expedition to the North Pacific 1853–1856*. Princeton, NJ: Princeton University Press, 1947.

Craig, Albert M. *Chōshū in the Meiji Restoration*. Cambridge, MA: Harvard University Press, 1967.

Crawcour, E. Sydney. "Economic Change in the Nineteenth Century." In *The Economic Emergence of Modern Japan*, edited by Kozo Yamamura. New York: Cambridge University Press, 1997.

David Rumsey Map Collection. *Sekai zu* (World Map), Japanese historical maps. Accessed February 6, 2019. http://japanmaps.davidrumsey.com.

de Bary, Wm. Theodore, ed. *Sources of Japanese Tradition*. Vol II. New York: Columbia University Press, 1958.

de Coningh, C. T. Assendelft. *A Pioneer in Yokohama*. Translated and edited by Martha Chaiklin. Indianapolis: Hackett Publishing, 2012.

Dore, Ronald. *Education in Tokugawa Japan*. Berkeley: University of California Press, 1965.

Duiker, William. *Contemporary World History*. 6th ed. Boston: Wadsworth Press, 2014.

Duus, Peter. *Modern Japan*. Boston: Houghton Mifflin Company, 1998.

———. *The Japanese Discovery of America: A Brief History with Documents*. New York: Bedford/St. Martin's, 1997.

Feifer, George. *Breaking Open Japan: Commodore Perry, Lord Abe, and American Imperialism in 1853*. New York: Smithsonian Books, 2006.

Fujimori Taiga. *Ishinshi* [A History of the Meiji Restoration]. Vol. 1. Tokyo: Meiji Shoin, 1939.

Gerstle, Andrew, ed. *18th Century Japan: Culture and Society*. New York: Routledge Press, 1989.

Greenberg, Amy S. *Manifest Manhood and the Antebellum American Empire*. Cambridge: Cambridge University Press, 2005.

Griffis, William Elliot. *Townsend Harris: First American Envoy in Japan*. London: Sampson Low, Marston & Company, 1895.

Gubbins, John Harrington. *The Progress of Japan, 1853–1871*. Oxford: Oxford University Press, 1912.

Hane Mikiso. *Peasants, Rebels, Women, and Outcastes: The Underside of Modern Japan*. New York: Pantheon, 1982.

Hauser, William B. *Economic Institutional Change in Tokugawa Japan: Osaka and the Kinai Cotton Trade*. Cambridge: Cambridge University Press, 1974.

Hayami Akira. *Population, Family and Society in Pre-Modern Japan*. Folkstone, UK: Brill/Global Oriental Press, 2010.

Heine, W. "First Landing at Gorahama." U.S. Library of Congress. Accessed January 8, 2019. https://www.loc.gov/item/2003655312/.

Hiroshi Mitani. *Escape from Impasse: The Decision to Open Japan*. Tokyo: International House of Japan, 2006.

Ikoku Ochibe Kago [A Basket of Fallen Leaves from a Foreign Country]. Tokyo: Bigakudo, 1854.

Kaempfer, Englebert, *The History of Japan: Giving an Account of the Ancient and Present State and Government of That Empire; of Its Temples, Palaces, Castles, and Other Buildings, of Its Metals, Minerals, Trees, Plants, Animals, Birds and Fishes, of the Chronology and Succession of the Emperors, Ecclesiastical and Secular, of the Original Descent, Religions, Customs, and Manufactures of the Natives, and of Their Trade and Commerce with the Dutch and Chinese: Together with a Description of the Kingdom of Siam*. Translated by J. G. Scheuchzer. London: Thomas Woodward and Charles Davis, 1728.

Kazui Tashiro and Susan Downing Videen. "Foreign Relations During the Edo Period: Sakoku Reexamined." *Journal of Japanese Studies* 8, no. 2 (1982): 284–306.

Kume Kunitake, comp. *The Iwakura Embassy: A True Account of the Ambassador Extraordinary and Plenipotentiary's Journey of Observation Through the United States and Europe*. Vol. 1, translated by Martin Collcutt. Princeton, NJ: Princeton University Press, 2002.

Lanman, Charles, ed. *The Japanese in America*. London: Longmans, Green, Reader, and Dyer, 1872.

Long, David Foster. *Sailor-Diplomat: A Biography of Commodore James Biddle, 1783–1848*. Boston: Northeastern University Press, 1983.

Lu, David J. *Japan: A Documentary History*. New York: M. E. Sharpe, 1997.

McClain, James L. "Failed Expectations: Kaga Domain on the Eve of the Meiji Restoration," *The Journal of Japanese Studies* 14, no. 2 (Summer 1988): 403–447.

McLaren, W. W. *Japanese Government Documents*. Tokyo: Asiatic Society of Japan, 1914.

Medzini, Meron. *French Policy in Japan during the Closing Years of the Tokugawa Regime*. Cambridge, MA: East Asian Research Center, Harvard University, 1971.

Miller, John H. "Social Disorder in Late Tokugawa Japan." PhD diss., Princeton University, 1975.

Nishikawa Shunsaku. "The Economy of Chōshū on the Eve of Industrialization." *The Economic Studies Quarterly*, 38, no. 4 (December 1987): 324–325.

Ohno Kenichi. *The History of Japanese Economic Development: Origins of Private Dynamism*. New York: Routledge Press, 2018.

Perry, Matthew Calbraith, Francis L. Hawks, George Jones, and A. O. P. Nicholson. *Narrative of the Expedition of an American Squadron to the China Seas and Japan, Performed in the Years 1852, 1853 and 1854, Under the Command of Commodore M. C. Perry, United States Navy*. Washington, DC: A. O. P. Nicholson, 1856.

"Report of Captain Lindenberg, of the Russian American Company's Ship *Prince Menchikoff*, to the Commander of the Colony of Sitka, October 17, 1852." *New York (Weekly) Tribune*, December 24, 1853.

Roberts, Luke S. "A Petition for a Popularly Chosen Council of Government in Tosa in 1787." *Harvard Journal of Asiatic Studies* 57, no. 2 (December 1997): 575–596.

Rubinger, Richard. *Popular Literacy in Early Modern Japan*. Honolulu: University of Hawaii Press, 2007.

Samuels, Richard J. *"Rich Nation, Strong Army": National Security and the Technical Transformation of Japan*. Ithaca, NY: Cornell University Press, 1994.

Smith, Thomas C. *The Agrarian Origins of Modern Japan*. Palo Alto, CA: Stanford University, 1959.

———. *Native Sources of Japanese Industrialization, 1750–1920*. Berkeley: University of California Press, 1989.

Soranaka Isao. "The Kansei Reforms—Success or Failure," *Monumenta Nipponica* 33, no. 2 (Summer 1978): 151–164.

Stearns, Peter. *World History in Brief: Major Patterns of Change and Continuity*. 8th ed. Upper Saddle River, NJ: Pearson, 2013.

Toby, Ronald P. *State and Diplomacy in Early Modern Japan: Asia in the Development of the Tokugawa Bakufu*. Princeton, NJ: Princeton University Press, 1984.

Tomes, Robert. *The Americans in Japan: An Abridgement of the Government Narrative of the U.S. Expedition*. New York: D. Appleton & Co, 1857.

"Treaties and Conventions Concluded Between Japan and Foreign Nations, Together with Notifications & Regulations Made from Time to Time." *Daily Japan Herald* (Yokohama), 1871.

Umihara Tōru. *Yoshida Shōin and the Shōka Sonjuku: The True Spirit of Education*. Vol. 2. Bloomington: Indiana University Center for Research on Japanese Educational History and East Asian Studies Center, 2000.

Van Bergen, Robert. *The Story of Japan*. New York: The American Book Company, 1897.

Vlastos, Stephen. *Peasant Protest and Uprisings in Tokugawa Japan*. Berkeley: University of California Press, 1990.

Walworth, Arthur. *Black Ships Off Japan: The Story of Commodore Perry's Expedition*. New York: A. A. Knopf, 1946.

Westney, D. E. *Imitation and Innovation: The Transfer of Western Organizational Patterns to Meiji Japan*. Cambridge, MA: Harvard University Press, 1987.

———. "The Emulation of Western Organizations in Meiji Japan." In *Meiji Japan: The Emergence of the Meiji State*, edited by Peter Kornicki. London: Routledge Press, 1999.

Wiley, Peter Booth. *Yankees in the Land of the Gods: Commodore Perry and the Opening of Japan*. New York: Penguin Books, 1991.
Yasutada Teruoka. "The Pleasure Quarters and Tokugawa Culture." In *18th Century Japan: Culture and Society*, edited by Andrew Gerstle. New York: Routledge Press, 1989.
Yokoi Shōnan. "Kokuze Sanron. The Three Major Problems of State Policy." Edited and translated by Dixon Y. Miyauchi. *Monumenta Nipponica* 23, no. 1–2, (1968): 156–186.

INDEX